CLIMATE CHANGE – A CHALLENGE FOR EUROPE AND CYPRUS

D1785012

CLIMATE CHANGE –
A CHALLENGE FOR
EUROPE AND CYPRUS

Results of the Second Conference on Sustainability of the German-Cypriot Forum in Cooperation with Friends of Nature Cyprus in November 2009 in Nicosia

Edited by Engin Karatas and Eckart Kuhlwein (German-Cypriot Forum)

© 2010 Engin Karatas and Eckart Kuhlwein
Publisher: tredition GmbH
Co-Publisher: rotation
Book typesetting: Tamara Pirschalawa
Cover picture: Sigrid Kuhlwein

Printed in Germany

ISBN: 978-3-86850-819-2

The conference was supported by German Federal Environmental Foundation (DBU) and the German Foreign Office (Auswärtiges Amt).

Contents

FOREWORD OF ECKART KUHLWEIN

Chairman of the German-Cypriot Forum

Dear friends in cyprus and from other European Countries,

in the beginning of the 21st century climate change has become a central challenge of global policy making and in terms of sustainable development. Unless it can be stopped in time, there will be incalculable consequences for the economic and social development of a globalized society.

The member states of the European Union and the EU itself has to come forward in the vanguard of climate policy. Industrialized national economies should prove their will to take action through substantial reductions and financing offers of their own for relevant measures in the countries of the south. This ought to be a key issue at the imminent Copenhagen Climate Summit. Climate protection requires not only the use of renewable energy sources, energy saving and improvement of energy efficiency; but also mitigation of adverse impacts through nature conservation and preservation of biodiversity. In this context, better water management, regulated waste management (recycling), CO_2 sinks, e.g. in the form of managed forests, as well as an improved environmental education play an essential part.

With our project "Climate Change: Challenges for Europe and Cyprus" we follow the UN conference on environment and development (UNCED) at Rio de Janeiro in June 1992 and its call for sustainable development. The Cyprus initiatives from the civil society should strengthen an ongoing process which entails that: economic policy considers ecological and social consequences, tourism policy respects nature, and agricultural policy takes into better account the protection of the environment. This integrated political approach can also be found in the relevant EU documents. The German-Cypriot Forum was successful at winning "Friends of Nature Cyprus" as a cooperation partner. A further partner is the "Cyprus Environmental Stakeholder Forum".

Please have a look at our conference-website www.cyprus-climate-conference.info. You will find more than 800MB of additional information about the findings of our conference. One article will be the Greenline-Project by Dr. Anna Grichting, architect and landscape planner, whose project aspires to make the buffer zone a "laboratory of ecological territorial planning and a catalyst for lasting peace". It takes into account the concept of a European Green Belt – an initiative focusing on the former border areas along the „Iron Curtain" where, due to decades of non-cultivation and isolation a corridor of valuable biotopes has developed that today is protected by conservation laws.

Eckart Kuhlwein

PREFACE OF ENGIN KARATAS

Secretary of the German-Cypriot Forum

Climate Change – A Real Threat to Human Mankind

Climate change is already happening and represents one of the biggest environmental, social and economic threats the planet faces. The warming of the climate system is unequivocal: increases in global average air and ocean temperatures, extensive melting of ice and snow, and a slow but steady rise of the global sea level. The expected global warming for the next 40 years is likely to trigger serious consequences for mankind and all other life forms: flooding and droughts, storms and hurricanes, food and water shortages at a more elevated frequency as well as a sea level rise, that puts coastal areas and islands like Cyprus in danger.

The Fourth Assessment Report of the Intergovernmental Panel on Climate Change (IPCC) explains: With a certainty of more than 90 percent it is for sure that emissions of heat-trapping gases produced by human activities have caused "most of the observed increase in globally averaged temperatures since the mid-20th century." It is absolutely clear that both, warming as well as cooling, has always occurred in the past, and long before humans started to emit gases or cut down forests. Many natural factors – the so called "natural climate drivers" – are influencing Earth's climate, e. g. volcanic eruptions, intensified sun activities, or natural occurring heat-trapping gases in the atmosphere.

The questions therefore is: How can scientists be sure that today's warming is primarily caused by mankind as a result of burning coal, oil, and gas or cutting down our forests?

There are some means to identify the human involvement in the carbon overload: Carbon molecules that come from gas, fossil fuels and deforestation is "lighter" than from those sources existing naturally. Therefore, when humans burn coal, oil and gas (fossil fuels) for whatever purpose, they leave fingerprints by emitting a "lighter" type of dioxide. The amount of this type of carbon in the atmosphere has increased in the last four decades significantly.

The average raise in temperature cannot be explained sufficiently enough by natural changes. Scientists using elaborated models are not able to accurately project the future climate, when models only take recorded "natural climate drivers" into account. These kinds of models cannot accurately reproduce the observed warming of the last six decades. Only models that include "human-induced climate drivers" can accurately grasp recent temperature increases. Compared to one another, the "human-induced climate drivers" are by far the largest "climate change drivers". The atmosphere in the lower-level – which contains the carbon load – is expanding. In recent decades the boundary between the lower atmosphere (troposphere) and the higher atmosphere (stratosphere) has shifted upward. The change was most likely induced by heat-trapping gases, which were accumulated in the lower atmosphere: As the lower atmosphere heats up it expands, too (it is comparable with the warming of the air in a balloon).

This means: The Earth is heating up. The early warning signs of global climate change are for example spreading diseases, earlier spring arrival and of course warmer weather and heat waves. Global warming can be considered as one of the most serious challenges facing us today. In order to protect the economic well-being and health of current and future generations, we urgently must reduce our emissions of heat-trapping gases by using the know-how, technologies, and practical solutions already at our disposal.

There are solutions to global warming available to us today and it's time we put them to use. The amount of heat-trapping gases that we emit into the atmosphere can be reduced by these solutions. Among these solutions are ways of reducing the amount of coal, oil and gas we use to generate electricity or to produce power for our vehicles. Also, the protecting of forests, which store carbon in their biomass, is highly relevant.

The way we live today – how we invest, use energy, organize transport and treat forests – will certainly determine the climate change and – therefore – our common future. This book confronts the most urgent questions facing us now from a general and also from a Cyprus' specific point of view:

What is climate change and what definitions do exist;

what are the environmental, social and economic impacts of the change;

what can be done to reduce emissions, at what cost; how can the world adapt;

what does all this mean for corporations, governments and individuals?

Furthermore, the outstanding tableau of authors from Europe and Cyprus brings the right expertise to have an insight view into the challenges the Mediterranean island's nature is already facing in the context of climate change. This book is the result of the second "Conference on Sustainability" of the German-Cypriot Forum in Cooperation with Friends of Nature Cyprus, which took place in November 2009 in Cyprus.

WATER MANAGEMENT IN CYPRUS AND THE IMPLEMENTATION OF THE EU WATER FRAME-WORK DIRECTIVE

Sofoclis Aletraris, Director of the Water Development Department, Ministry of Agriculture, Natural Resources and Environment, Republic of Cyprus

Abstract

The purpose of this presentation is to illustrate in a simplified manner how Cyprus has managed water over the years as well as the measures taken to relieve the recent water crisis. A brief overview of how the European Union addresses the challenge of water scarcity and droughts and the progress of implementation of the EU Water Framework Directive in Cyprus will also be presented.

1. Introduction

Over the coming decades, climate change will have a significant impact on the quality and availability of water resources both within Europe and globally. Limited water availability already poses a problem in many parts of the world and climate change is expected to make matters worse. According to the Intergovernmental Panel on Climate Change, climate change would bring water scarcity to between 1.1 and 3.2 billion people if temperatures rose by 2° to 3° C. Drought affected areas are likely to increase in extent.

At European Union level, the number of areas and people affected by droughts went up by almost 20% between 1976 and 2006. One of the most widespread droughts occurred in 2003 when over 100 million people (20%) and a third of the EU territory were affected. The cost of the damage to the European economy was at least €

14

8.7 billion. The total cost of droughts over the past thirty years amounts to € 100 billion.

In these circumstances, it has become an EU priority to devise effective drought risk management strategies.

2. Addressing the Challenge of Water Scarcity and Droughts in the European Union

Against the above background, on 18 July 2007, the European Commission adopted a Communication addressing the challenge of water scarcity and droughts in the European Union. The Communication provides a fundamental and well-developed first set of policy options for future action, within the framework of EU water management principles, policies and objectives. It also states a clear commitment from the EU, as a whole, to jointly establish the adequate conditions to implement the foreseen actions and to develop further knowledge.

2.1 Policy options

The set of proposed policies on water aims to move the EU towards a water-efficient and water-saving economy.

At the heart of the policy options is the need to put the right price on water. The "user pays" principle needs to become the rule regardless of where the water is taken from. Efforts to introduce compulsory metering programmes are thus essential. Water saving and water efficiency measures need to be promoted given that there is a tremendous potential for water savings in the European Union. While it is estimated that approximately 20 per cent of the water available is wasted, recent data indicate that it could go up as high as 40 per cent. Therefore, substantial changes must be made on how water is channelled to users and how it is used. It is easy, for example, to promote the installation of water saving devices on taps, shower heads, and toilets.

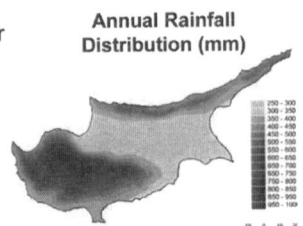
On a larger scale, a proper allocation of water use between economic sectors needs to be considered. Policy making should be based on a clear "water hierarchy" meaning that water saving must become the priority. Effective water pricing and cost-effective measures for improving water demand management should also be considered before opting for additional water infrastructures. Accordingly, the integration of water sustainability and sustainable land use must become an integral part of policy making in areas such as agriculture and tourism. All activities should be adapted to the amount of water available locally.

3. Addressing the Challenge of Water Scarcity
   and Droughts in Cyprus

In Cyprus, most of the water demand management measures presented in the Communication have been applied, or they are being applied, with the problem of water scarcity remaining, despite the many successful demand management and costly supply enhancement measures implemented.

Water scarcity has always been a serious problem for Cyprus, which together with Malta are the "water poor" countries of Europe with the lowest water availability per capita.

Like other Mediterranean countries, Cyprus has a semi-arid climate and limited water resources which depend mainly on rainfall. However, rainfall in Cyprus is unevenly distributed with considerable regional variations, water resources are scarce and expensive to exploit and droughts occur frequently.

Climate change is already affecting Cyprus in a number of ways. Statistical analysis reveals a stepped drop of precipitation in Cyprus in the early 70's, which persists, while climate models for this region also predict a rise in temperature and an increase in the intensity and frequency of extreme drought events. These conditions, coupled with increased water demands, are worsening the water scarcity problem on the island.

3.1 Water use

Domestic use and irrigation are the two main water-consuming sectors in Cyprus.

Irrigated agriculture accounts for about 69% of total water demand and the domestic sector, which includes the tourist and industrial sector for 25%. The remaining 6% is used for other industrial (1%) and environmental purposes (5%). The tourist demand accounts for about 5% of total. It should be noted however that the above figures refer to water needs, which are rarely satisfied. For example, since 1996, the water demand for irrigated agriculture was satisfied only once, during the hydrological year of 2004, when all dams over spilled.

3.2 Water resources management in Cyprus – Track record

Over the years, the Government of Cyprus has come to realize that water, as a limited resource, must be carefully managed and that simply attempting to satisfy increasing demand by increasing the supply does not provide a sustainable solution. Hence, a more integrated and sustainable approach to water resources management has always been pursued, tackling the water issue in terms of quantity, quality, health, conservation and protection and economics.

Strategic planning of water resources management consists of two categories of measures:

a) long-term actions to improve the reliability of each system to meet future demands under scarcity conditions and

b) short-term actions, which try to face a particular drought event within the existing framework of infrastructures and management policies.

In order to cope with annual drought events, the Government applies a Drought Mitigation and Response Plan in all Government Water Works (GWW) on a yearly basis, depending on prevailing climatic conditions. It includes different restrictions to water use, and other water demand and supply management measures.

Water from the GWW is allocated to different uses, giving priority to the domestic water sector (including tourism) due to its great importance for welfare and public health. The remaining quantity is allocated to agriculture using a quota system, in combination with penalty charges for over-consumption. According to the scenarios applied, the available quantity is allocated to farms depending on the crop and area irrigated. Over-consumption is charged with a rate that is a multiple of the usual tariff and in cases of further use the supply is disconnected. The measure is applied almost every year, with the exemption of some rare years with satisfactory rainfall-inflow to the dams.

Regarding the long-term actions, the Republic of Cyprus, embarked during the late sixties on the implementation of a Water Master Plan with the objective to satisfy, in a sustainable way, the different users of water and to safeguard human and other life.

Several measures were used to increase availability of water and decrease water demand.

On the supply side the dams' capacity was increased from 6 million cubic meters in 1960 to 327,5 million cubic meters today. Boreholes were drilled for domestic and irrigation purposes and water treatment plants and recharge works were constructed.

On the demand side the installation of improved on farm irrigation systems was encouraged, the construction of modern, efficient conveyance and distribution systems with minor losses was promoted and water charges were imposed both for domestic water supply and for irrigation water.

Nevertheless, despite the significant efforts and measures taken, the available water was not enough to satisfy the water demand. An analysis of the situation indicated that water shortage was due to a great extent to the climatic change, which caused a reduction of approximately 20% in the precipitation and resulted in a 40% reduction in surface runoff. In addition more frequent occurrence of extreme drought events is experienced. Furthermore there was also a rapid increase in the population and number of tourist arrivals in Cyprus, which placed additional demands for water.

The groundwater resources of the island have been the most obvious and easily accessible sources of water for many years and as a result in the attempt to meet the increasing water demand or to mitigate drought effects, they have been heavily over pumped. This has led to seawater intrusion of many coastal aquifers and deterioration of both quality and quantity of groundwater.

The above conditions forced the Government of Cyprus in 1997, to turn to sea water desalination for augmenting potable water supply and increasing water security so that every person has access to safe water. Currently one mobile and two permanent desalination plants are in operation and additional desalination plants are planned to be constructed in the next couple of years with the objective to eliminate the dependency of the potable water on rainfall.

Despite the environmental and financial costs from the operation of a desalination plant, experience has shown that desalination remains the only means of achieving water security and independence of the domestic water supply from the climatic behaviour.

In the meantime the importance of other non-conventional water resources such as recycling of treated municipal effluents had already been recognized and begun to be developed. Recycled water for irrigation and recharge purposes is a growing resource in Cyprus. Reuse schemes using treated sewage effluent are now operational and many more are under study or construction.

Today, 14,5 million cubic meters of recycled water are being produced from tertiary treatment. More than 50% is used for irrigation of agricultural crops, either directly or through recharge of aquifers. They cover needs of the existing water balance and replace equal quantities of good quality water. The rest is used for recharge and for irrigation of recreational areas (landscaping, hotel gardens etc). Annual water recycling is estimated to increase to 52 million cubic meters by 2012 (28,5% of agricultural water demand).

On the other hand, a fundamental condition for the exercise and application of a sustainable water policy is the management of the demand of water. In Cyprus, water demand management has always been an integral part of the policy on water and demand management measures such as metering of water consumption and water charges on a volumetric basis, programs to reduce distribution losses, improved on farm irrigation systems, measures to promote a water-saving culture and efficiency of water use, water rationing during periods of drought, subsidies for saving potable water and many more, have been a tradition of the water authorities in Cyprus.

It is worth noting that the infrastructure and water demand management measures described above have mostly been funded through the National Budget and for a number of years the funds allocated for water development constituted approximately one fifth of the Development Budget of the Republic of Cyprus.

The 2007 value of the water infrastructure investments (Government Water Works) at a rate of 7,5% was estimated at €2,58 billion. Considering the size of the country (geography, economy, population) the above figures show how vital and expensive is water development in water scarce regions particularly in islands. It should also be noted that a considerable proportion of the above investment was put in water efficiency infrastructure such as the installation of advanced distribution networks and telemetry systems.

Finally Cyprus is progressing towards full implementation of the Water Framework Directive (WFD) and is totally committed to the efficient and effective implementation of its principles and provisions.

The WFD, which came into force in December 2000, represents an important step towards sustainable use of water resources in Europe. Its key aims are:

- to expand water protection to all waters: inland and coastal surface waters and groundwater,

- to achieve "good status" for all waters by 2015,

- to base water management on river basins,

- to combine emission limit values with environmental quality standards,

- to ensure that water prices provide adequate incentives for water users to use water resources efficiently,

- to involve citizens more closely and to streamline legislation.

The WFD provides for a number of deadlines by which Member States have to fulfill particular obligations and report their achievement to the European Commission. The key actions that Member States need to take are as follows:

- to transpose the WFD into national law and identify the River Basin Districts (RBDs) and competent authorities by December 2003,

- to characterize river basin districts in terms of pressures, impacts and economics of water uses, including a register of protected areas by December 2004,

- to make operational monitoring programs and publish for consultation a work program for the production of the first River Basin Management Plans (RBMPs) by December 2006,

- to publish for consultation an interim overview of the significant water management issues in each RBD by December 2007,

- to present draft RBMPs to the public by December 2008,

- to finalize RBMPs for each RBD including a Program of Measures by December 2009,

- to implement water pricing policies that enhance the sustainability of water resources by December 2010,

- to make operational all the measures established under the Program of Measures by December 2012 and

- to achieve the environmental objectives (good status) by 2015.

Cyprus has fulfilled all its obligations up to the end of 2007 and using Consultancy Services is proceeding with the preparation of the River Basin Management Plans and the Programme of Measures. A specific Drought Management Plan to supplement WFD river basin management plan will also be developed.

A six month public consultation on the Draft RBMP according to Article 14 of the WFD is expected to begin in February 2010 and the whole work is expected to be completed by March 2011.

Cyprus was not able to meet the December 2008 deadline for the preparation of the Draft RBMP due to legal issues arisen in relation to the tenders. The Water Development Department was not in a position to act towards the preparation of the draft Plan until the Decision of the Court. The issue was resolved in December 2008 and the contract was eventually signed on 8th December 2008.

Consultancy Services are also currently in progress for the implementation of Article 9 of the WFD which establishes the requirement to implement cost recovery, including environmental and resource costs, the polluter pays principle and incentive pricing by 2010.

The Contract, which was signed in February 2008, is expected to be completed by the end of 2009. Public consultation will follow.

4. Current water situation in Cyprus

During the past year, Cyprus was faced with one of the most acute and prolonged droughts since the beginning of the twentieth century, with very severe water shortages and socio-economic and environmental impacts.

The 2008 winter was extremely dry, the second driest since 1901 and the inflow to the reservoirs was only 18,7 mcm of water, the lowest in the last seventeen years. As a result, the water reserves of underground aquifers have been drastically reduced and water storage in the dams has reached dangerously low levels.

In response, a drastic Drought Mitigation and Response Plan has been applied with a series of emergency measures. These include among others:

- The transfer of potable water from Greece, using tankers.

- An almost 100% ban on the supply of water to agriculture through the Government Water Works.

- Strict restrictions on the supply of drinking water to households, limiting the supply to only 36 hours per week.

- Extension of the existing desalination plants and installation of mobile ones.

- treatment of the raw water of the Garillis aquifer in Limassol to potable water.

- Use of new boreholes and purchase of water from private boreholes to reinforce domestic water supply.

- Intensification of the water saving promotion campaigns and continuation of the financial incentives schemes for saving potable water.

In addition the following measures are currently in progress or being planned:

- Domestic water supply enhancement measures such as construction of three new permanent desalination plants in Limassol and Paphos and Kannaviou Treatment Plant.

- Replacement and improvement of domestic water supply networks in rural areas. (The available amount in the national budget for 2009 amounts to approximately €15 million and involves 150 projects, while the funds allocated for the period 2001-2008 are estimated at approximately €60 million).

- Study for exploring the possibility of rainwater utilization.

- Solea Valley Irrigation Project for irrigation water use improvement.

- Implementation of Urban Waste Water Treatment Directive 91/271/EEC and use of recycled water for irrigation.

- Other environmental protection and demand management measures.

Furthermore to help respond to the crisis the Government of Cyprus also applied for financial assistance from the EU Solidarity Fund, where the European Commission agreed to grant €7,6 million in aid. The aid will mainly help reimburse costs of emergency measures, such as the transport of water from Greece. This is the first time the Solidarity Fund was used to provide financial aid for emergency measures in response to an exceptional drought.

This year the situation has improved with rainfall reaching 105% of normal. The inflow to the reservoirs was 97,2 million cubic meters of water enabling the government to reduce the restrictions on the supply of drinking water to households from 30% to 15% and to provide some quantities of water to agriculture.

5. Conclusions

Our vision on water is to provide sustainably to the people of Cyprus sufficient, safe, clean, healthy and reliable water for domestic and irrigation needs and for the environment.

The future presents many challenges for Cyprus. Rapid social changes, efforts for economic development, climate change, water scarcity and droughts and escalating water demands in a continuously changing environment, will place additional pressures on the limited water resources of the island.

The Government of Cyprus is fully aware of the challenges ahead and through an integrated multi-objective approach for water management is taking all necessary measures to ensure water security now and in the future. The road will not be easy, but there are no alternatives.

WATER MANAGEMENT IN CYPRUS AND THE IMPLE-MENTATION OF THE EU WATER FRAMEWORK DIRECTIVE – PART II: A GERMAN NGO PERSPECTIVE

Michael Bender, Green League – German Environmental NGO (Grüne Liga)

1. Introduction

One of the main instruments for the water management in the European Union if not the most relevant is the European water framework directive. On the wider European perspective the UNECE Convention on the protection and use of transboundary water causes and international lakes and plays a major role.

EEB/WWF: 5 key priorities

Five priorities for better water management:
- Transparent and publicly owned water management
- Reducing wastage and using water well
- More space for living rivers
- Healthy, safe water for people and nature
- Visionary and adaptive water policies

WILL THE EU'S WATERS BE REVIVED?

GRÜNE LIGA Netzwerk Ökologischer Bewegungen

May 2009

The Convention on the Protection and Use of Transboundary Watercourses and International Lakes was done at Helsinki on 17 March 1992. It intends to strengthen national measures for the protection and ecologically sound management of transboundary surface waters and groundwaters. The parties of the treaty are obliged to prevent, control and reduce water pollution from point and non-point sources.

The Convention also includes provisions for monitoring, research and development, consultations, warning and alarm systems, mutual assistance, institutional arrangements, and the exchange and protection of information, as well as public access to information.

Under the convention the Protocol on Water and Health was adopted in London on 17 June 1999. Its importance is underlined by the fact that in the European Region, 120 million people do not have access to safe drinking-water, and even more lack access to sanitation, resulting in waterborne diseases such as diarrhoeal diseases, hepatitis A and typhoid fever (170,000 estimated cases in 2006). Microbial contamination has been recognized as the prime concern throughout the European Region. Chemical pollution is localized but may also have a significant impact on health.

2. The European Water framework directive Environmental Goals of the WFD

The central objective of the Water Framework Directive (WFD) is to achieve "good status" for surface and ground water by 2015. With its ambitious environmental goals and targets for comprehensive consideration of biological parameters, the WFD introduces the ecosystem approach to European waters: water management must concern itself with the goal of preserving water as a habitat for aquatic flora and fauna, which is a reference point for a "good" and natural state of water. The concept of good status for waters is derived from components of a water body's ecological and chemical status. The directive also lays down a general non-deterioration obligation for all waters. A key criterion for assessing the condition of groundwater is the degree of human intervention in it and the level of impairment of ecosystems dependent on it caused by this intervention. An EU-wide mandatory threshold for nitrate (50 mg / l) and for pesticides is used. A number of pollutants, the so-called

Priority Substances, are subject to special regulations-in a daughter directive-which combine emissions limits and imissions quality targets in order to reduce their concentration.

2.1 Basic Principles in Implementing the WFD

The WFD introduces integrated management within river basins, in either large basins (e.g. Rhine, Elbe, Danube) or several neighboring small rivers (e.g. Warnow/Peene), with an obligation to transboundary cooperation. Through a joint implementation strategy (Common Implementation Strategy, CIS) the activities of the member states are supported by the EU Commission and Water Directors, through the use of "guidance" documents and similar strategies. Environmental organizations participate in this process mainly through the European Environmental Bureau (EEB) in Brussels and WWF. In Germany, the environmental ministries of the individual federal states are responsible for implementing the WFD. The states mostly coordinate their activities within river regions and nationwide through the LAWA, the state/federal Water Working Group. In the international river commissions, where along the Danube, Elbe, Oder and Rhine the WFD implementation will be coordinated across borders, environmental organizations have observer status. The WFD, as the first EU-wide mandatory regulation scheme, explicitly uses economic instruments to implement environmental objectives. In particular, measures should be combined as efficiently as possible. RBMP will require a long-term economic analysis of water.

2.2 River Basin Management Plans

The action frameworks to improve the situation of European waters are outlined in River Basin Management Plans (RBMP) that have been drafted from the end of 2006 to the end of 2009. The guidelines of the WFD focus less on preliminary aspects such as content, format and design, but rather mainly on the objective of obtaining good water status. It is obvious that this objective will only be achieved by using a broad palette of instruments, from individual technical endeavors to an overarching transformation of agro-environmental politics. Action should be taken now. We have the chance to address high-impact structures such as dams and dikes whose technical utilities have expired. A small step, such as uncovering piped waters running through farmland, is one example of an economically advantageous alternative to reconstruction. The regulation of exemptions is built into the RBMP, in particular the designation of "heavily modified water bodies". Classification as a HMWB will be justified in the high cost of improvement or, as the case may be, limits of technical feasibility.

2.3 Public Participation under WFD Article 14

Public consultation takes place in three stages (see schedule below). Beyond the mandatory distribution of information and consultation, competent authorities are obliged to encourage "active involvement" of the public. The opportunities of active participation reflect higher quality and readier acceptance of the resulting plans, and also the integration of actors, allowing them to implement measures within their own capacities. Environmental organizations, especially those with conservation objectives should insist on the "no deterioration" clause and are encouraged to demand that exceptions remain exceptions, and must not become the rule.

3. Public Participation in Forming a Management Plan for Water

3.1 Europe's Water is an Imminent Concern

Reaching good, healthy conditions in most German rivers will only be possible through various and extensive measures. To the level of necessity of these measures is clarified by a survey taken in 2005, which gives a tentative estimate: at most 60% of water bodies in Germany fail to meet good status. Deficits within the morphologic structures of water bodies and eutrophication are among the leading causes of poor water quality.

Key steps:

- Improvement of the hydromorphology and restoration of habitats

- Assurance of biological permeability

- Natural development of floodplains

- Reduction of nutrient inflow, especially from agriculture

- Reduction of toxin inflow

3.2 Nature Conservation as a Goal of the Water Management

Nature protection is an explicit goal of the WFD. In water-related, protected areas, especially those within the Natura 2000-Network, conservation goals are at the same time goals of the WFD. Water management is thus obliged to contribute to the achievement of the considered nature conservation objectives.

As a general rule, the hydrologic development objectives of the WFD are consistent with the concepts of ecological protection, and the integration of floodplains needs to be a central issue. From the perspective of nature conservation, another key concern is that the WFD mandates the improvement of the state of groundwater-dependent ecosystems and wetlands.

Floodplains are part of the river structure. Without "lateral connectivity," it will be hard to achieve good status.

4. Fields of Conflict

The ecological development goals of the WFD are in many cases in conflict with agricultural practices and flood prevention measures as well as the use of water bodies as waterways and for hydropower. These areas of conflict need to be taken into account as significant water management issues and regarded carefully. The

WFD establishes a framework for regulating necessary exemptions for all water uses.

An overwhelming portion of pollution comes from agricultural land and the maintenance of water by agriculture, entailing further ecological problems. In spite of the ambiguity of the EU Common Agricultural Policy, during discussions of available funds for water projects, it should be considered that much of the pollution which farming creates is heavily subsidized by the public. A stepwise solution to this, a polluter-pays approach, appears effective and needs to be considered in the context of cost efficiency. The contents of compensation-free, law abiding, "good farming" practices and their delineation from subsidies for avoiding environmental damage have hardly been discussed within the context of the WFD. Until May 2009, according to the Water Budget Act (WHG), the creation of flood control plans should be closely linked with RBMP and the drafts should be presented publicly. Especially on the Danube, Elbe and Oder, the use and maintenance of waterways, particularly within the framework of the EU's "Trans-European Networks," sometimes jeopardize the objectives of water and nature conservation. Unfortunately, the economic analysis carried out in advance of the draft RBMP provides no reliable economic data for traffic on these waterways, supplying no counterweight to water protection objectives.

5. Timeline for Implementing the WFD

- 2003 Transposing into national law and defining competent authorities
- 2004 Initial survey of water status in river basins (Report 2005)
- 2006 Establishment of monitoring networks
- 2006-09 Preparation of the River Basin Management Plans
    - Schedule and Work Program (2006)
    - Overview of the main water management issues (2007)

- draft of the plans and programs (2008) in consultation with the public, with a six-month deadline for submitting comments
- 2009 Completion of the RBMP
- 2009 Establishment of flood control plans in accordance with WHG
- 2009-12 Implementation of the Measures
- 2010 Effective water pricing
- 2015 Accomplishing the Environmental Goals
- Beginning of the Second Planning Cycle
- 2021 End 1. Extension time period
- 2027 End 2. Extension time period

6. The Green League Water Policy Office

6.1. EU and Nationwide Water Protection

The Green League Water Policy Office has been working for years on water issues with regional, state and international focuses. It leads nationwide information seminars for interested parties. The EU Water Framework Directive (WFD) formulates new objectives for the protection of rivers, lakes, coasts and groundwater. The Water Policy Office prepares "good practice examples" for renaturation and cooperation in the form of profiles. A related exhibition can be lent out. Regular publications include the bi-annual WRRL-*Info* newsletter as well as the monthly "Water Page" email. Further information is available on the website www.wrrl-info.de.

The Water Policy Office has been part of the Water Working Group of the European Environmental Bureau (EEB) for years and participated in the EU-wide drafting process for the EU Water Framework Directive and other European water legislation processes and has coordinated the intentions of German environmental organizations nationwide. Michael Bender represents the GREEN LEAGUE as an observer in the Assembly and WFD Working Group (Water

Framework Directive) of the International Commission for the Protection of the Elbe and the Elbe River Basin Community.

6.2. The GREEN LEAGUE's WFD Project

As part of the Federal Ministry of Environment and Federal Environment Agency funded project: WFD Implementation, we want to support water protection activities of environmental groups and provide arguments for the discussion of the River Basin Management Plans and the Programme of Measures. The core of our project is presenting good examples of water management in the form of informational profiles through which environmental groups and water authorities will be able to see a range of possible actions to meet the environmental objectives of the WFD.

7. Further fields of Action & Initiatives

7.1. Action Alliance against the Havel River Canalization

The GREEN LEAGUE Berlin is one of the cofounders of the "Alliance for Action Against the Havel River Canalization." The objectives of the project are the protection of the Havel landscape and stopping the transportation project "German Unity" No. 17, which proposes excessive construction in Berlin and the state of Brandenburg.

7.2. Berlin Water Roundtable

The Berlin Water Roundtable is a local network of representatives of different groups, initiatives, and interested citizens grouped together under the common theme that "Water belongs to us all – water is a human right." As a regional network, the Water Roundtable concentrates on the goal of ensuring transparency in water management and ensuring the end of the partial privatization of the Berlin water utilities. The GREEN LEAGUE was the key signature collector during the People's Initiative "End the Secret Contracts – We Berliners want our water back!"

7.3. German NGO-Forum on Environment and Development, WG Water

In the Water Working Group of the German NGO Forum on Environment and Development (FUE), environmental and development organizations work on water issues of international importance. The working themes include the human right to water, large dams and their consequences, the privatization of water management (with particular regard to the GATS negotiations at the WTO), and sustainable sanitation. The GREEN LEAGUE coordinates the work of these organizations in the WG Water of the FUE and in the German Nature Conservation Network (DNR).

8. German Forum on Development and Environment

8.1. Working Group on Water

Global water resources have always been an international issue for environmental and development negotiations. Controversies over water are the core of many disputes between states as well as those within states. Water resources lie at the interface between environment and development like no other issue, making the formation of the Forum's Water Working Group on February 7, 2001 all the more important. The WG has been active for years in the discussion group "Environmental Organizations and Water Management" founded by the German League for Nature and a number of interested, development-policy-focused NGOs as a means to come together from time to time and discuss cooperation opportunities.

The first field of action was the Bonn Freshwater Conference 2001. The German version of the resulting policy paper appeared as an updated edition in 2003 for the UN International Year of Freshwater, and is still the basis of the Water WG's self-understanding. The UN Year of Sanitation 2008 was cause for another policy paper and a number of related events.

8.2. Composition and Themes of the WG

In the Water WG, members of environmental and development groups work alongside foundations and representatives from trade unions. It is a common concern within the group to anchor sustainability criteria to European water management for the future in order to prevent them from being lost in a melee of privatization and market power concentration.

The WG devotes itself to supporting the human right to water. Some members of the WG participate in the work of the Sustainable Sanitation Alliance (Susana) and the GTZ ecosan Initiative for ecologically sound sanitation. Another focus of climate change and water includes among others the adaptation of water uses – in particular the question of CO_2 trading under the CDM (Clean Development Mechanism). The critical evaluation of large infrastructure projects, especially dams, also remains a topic of interest for the Water WG. Since 2002, the Water Working Group has interacted with representatives of water management and anti-globalization groups (UNSER Wasser Network, attac, etc.) in annual press conferences for the UN World Water Day against the privatization and liberalization of water management. The campaign "Protective dikes against water privatization" (see: More on the topic) presented a unified criticism of the privatization of municipal water utilities in Germany, with a critical analysis of water market liberalization efforts at the EU level and advocates water as a human right in the international sphere.

LANDSCAPES OF THE GREEN LINE.
HEALING THE RIFT.

Anna Grichting, Architect-Urbanist and Musician

Abstract

The Buffer Zone represents the physical rift and the psychological barrier that separates the Cypriot communities. In this negative space, the absence of human interventions has resulted in the preservation of endangered species and fragile ecosystems. Additionally, bi-communal and international environmental and cultural NGOs are collaborating across the Green Line on projects that relate to the construction of a sustainable and peaceful future for the island of Cyprus. How can these positive natural evolutions within the Buffer zone be preserved and the social collaborations across the dividing line be coordinated into a vision for the physical and social reconciliation of Cyprus? As an ecological and cultural landscape of memory and as a backbone for reunification, the Green Line can become an ecological corridor, a space of commemoration, containing new institutions for Cyprus, and implementing sustainable practices of planning, building and cultivating the land. Similar landscapes can be evoked that can inspire this vision including the Berlin Wall, the Iron Curtain Green Belt and the Korea Demilitarized Zone, and these precedents can help us to develop tools and instruments to implement this vision for a peaceful future.

1. From a deep wound to a beautiful scar.

The UN controlled Green Line occupies approximately 3% of the land mass of the island of Cyprus. Frozen in a military status quo for the past 35 years, this strip of land swallows up abandoned rural villages, agricultural lands that lie fallow, and stone buildings that crumble in the historic city of Nicosia. On the up side, this landscape has escaped the construction boom on both sides of the

Green Line, meadows have recovered from the contamination with pesticides and artificial fertilizers, hillside forests have been pre-served, and wildlife has been allowed to flourish. Similar to other military buffer zones worldwide, the most salient example being the Korean Demilitarized Zone, the Green Line has, due to its isolation, become really "green", that is, it has become a haven for biodiver-sity. The year 2010 being the International Year of Biodiversity - as designated by the United Nations - as well as the 60th anniversary of the foundation of the Republic of Cyprus, leads us to reflect on how this UN controlled Buffer Zone, could be transformed from a military dividing line into a new landscape of cultural and biological diversity[1], and this through a process that brings together the communities on both sides in a common project for an ecologically and socially sustainable future.

2. A vision for the Green Line

Lets us unbridle our imagination and imagine ourselves one day riding a bicycle along the former patrol path of the Green Line Buffer Zone in Cyprus, stopping at what was once a look-out tower to take in the landscape or to watch some rare birds, perhaps stay-ing overnight in one of the Green Line Eco-Lodges and stopping for nourishment in the taverns serving the organic produce of the Green Line farming communities. The more athletic amongst us might participate in the yearly Green Line Peace Marathon that begins and ends with a lap around the newly reconnected bastions of the Venetian Walls of the formerly divided city of Nicosia.

As a scholar, you could be drawn to the research institutes at the new Green campus, a bi-communal and international university in the former grounds of the Nicosia Airport and the UN protected area, a campus that is landscaped on the basis of a hydraulic grid

---

[1] Links between biological and cultural diversity-concepts, methods and experiences, Report of an International Workshop, UNESCO, Paris 2008

of water catchments and storm water basins and powered by re-newable energies. You would reach the campus from Nicosia or Ercan airport with the Green Line light rail, which traces the former tracks of the Famagusta-Nicosia-Lefke line, that disappeared in the 1950s.

As you ride along, your gaze would fall on buildings that reflect a new building code, with well-insulated walls, green roofs, water saving infrastructures, and many trees to provide shade. If you were not tempted by the light rail or bicycle ride, you might want to hire a solar car to discover the Green Line Trail, or a solar boat to cruise the shores of Varosha, the former ghost town on the East coast of the island near Famagusta.

Nature lovers could visit a Nature Field Station, a totally off-the-grid building nestled in one of the biodiversity hotspots of the protected areas of the Green Line. Here you would learn about the endangered species of Cyprus such as the Moufflon and the Monk Seal (both listed on the IUCN red list) which flourished in the abandoned mountain and marine landscapes of the Buffer Zone.[2] Approaching the city of Nicosia, you might visit the Cemetery of Monuments, where the relics and multiple manifestations of Greek and Turkish nationalism lay to rest. In the walled city of Nicosia, Art lovers will discover the new Green Line Gallery, that is housed in some of the formerly ruined buildings of the Green Line, in a structure that preserves the interconnections between the buildings that resulted from their transformation into bastions and bunkers. The architectural approach go the design of this gallery is similar to the restoration/reconstruction work of the British Architect, David Copperfield in Berlin's Neues Museum, which was damaged during the Second World War and which, through his daring design, preserves the buildings' sense of decay and records the patina of time.

A few steps along the Green Line Trail in the walled city, the New Museum of National Struggles conceptually connects and reinterprets the Greek and Turkish Cypriot National Struggle Museums which are located surprisingly close to each other in the walled city and which both currently focus on the wrongs done to them by the 'other' community. This museum for the Struggle *Against Nationalisms* exhibits historical memories of coexistence, which are intertwined with the recent memories of trauma, introducing a new multiplicitous narrative into the polarized landscape.

---

[2] The Mouflon was introduced in Cyprus during the Neolithic around 7000 years ago. This archaic species of sheep was sacred to the former inhabitants of Cyprus, and today it still appears on t bank notes and is on the logo of Cyprus Airways. It became nearly extinct, until breeding program reintroduced them in recent years. A community of 300 Moufflon was spotted in an abandoned village in the Buffer Zone.
The Mediterranean monk seal, the most threatened pinniped in the world, has been included by the Parties to the Barcelona Convention among their priority targets already since 1985 (Genoa Declaration). Monk seals have been sighted in the Turkish enclave of Kokkina on the West Coast of Cyprus, where the Green Line extends into the sea. Extremely shy mammals, the seals have benefited from the absence of fisherman and boats in the maritime Buffer Zone.

Finally, you could also participate in the construction of this vision and become a Shareholder of the Green Line by purchasing the Green Line Shares that would allow the purchase of land for public use in the Buffer Zone.

This vision for the Cyprus Green Line may seem fanciful, but it is not a utopia. It is grounded in the natural evolutions and resilience that have emerged within the Buffer Zone, as well as from the potential and existing collaborations between environmental, social and cultural organizations across the dividing line. As a laboratory for ecological planning and sustainable development for the Cyprus, this project for the Buffer Zone could benefit from economic incentives for "green growth" as well as paving the way for the development of new "green technologies and practices'.

3. "Borders are the scars of history"

This description of borders was made by Robert Schuman, a former French Statesman and one of the founding fathers of the European Union. Yet the Green Line of Cyprus cannot yet be considered a scar: It remains a physical and psychological wound, a military fault line, a territorial chasm that fragments landscapes and divides the societies. Regardless, the forces of Nature are inciting a process of cicatrisation, and revealing the Green Line as a potential haven of biodiversity and as an opportunity create a beautiful scar that will turn the marks of pain into the visible manifestations of a landscape of healing.

In the past, other geopolitical contour lines materialized as physical walls, defining frontiers and separating sedentary civilians from nomadic and so-called barbaric populations, or more recently, capitalist from communist societies. Hadrian's Wall, the Great Wall of China and the Iron Curtain were all transformed from being the edges of Empires to becoming backbones of cultural and natural tourism, developing nature trails, connecting heritage sites, and even organizing yearly marathons. The Annual Great Wall Marathon takes place on top of the Great Wall of China around in Beijing amidst spectacular scenery, and with its 3'700 steps, it is one of the more challenging world marathons. Hadrian's Wall has become a UNESCO World Heritage site that stretches along 130 kilometers across Great Britain and a National Trail has recently been inaugurated along its path following the remains of the wall both through built up areas and the National Park areas.

An ambitious environmental and memorial trail along the Iron Curtain - the pan-European Green Belt which runs for 8'500 kilometers from the Baltic Sea to the Mediterranean - aims to connect a valuable chain of biotopes that have become home to a number of endangered species also linking nature parks, biosphere reserves, and transboundary protected areas along its path. This variation of landscapes is linked by the former patrol path, which today serves bicycles, pedestrians and service vehicles.

An analog case to the Cyprus Green Line, the Korea Demilitarized Zone, which still remains an open wound between the two Koreas, has been described as a Garden of Eden, Walled Off Paradise or Involuntary Park. The demilitarized Zone of Korea (DMZ) is in fact one of the most highly militarized spots on the planet, yet this no-man's land has been out of bounds to humans for over 50 years. As a result a wild nature has evolved, and the strip of land measuring 250 kilometers by 4 kilometers has become the resting place of endangered migratory birds, for example the red-naped cranes, considered as sacred species and symbols of peace and longevity by both the North and South Koreans. As a final resting place for many Korean and international soldiers and civilian war victims, it is spiritually important to preserve the DMZ as a space of memory in which the victims are honored and remembered and this Garden of Eden has the potential to become the beautiful scar that participates in healing the peninsula of Korea and its people.

4. The United Nations Buffer Zone in Cyprus (UNBZ)

The Buffer Zone links a unique succession of landscapes and constitutes a cross-section of the many landscapes and ecologies of the island. From the deltas and sandy beaches of the east coast (Famagusta-Varosha), it connects with the rocky shores of the West coast (the Morphou Bay and Kokkina enclave), passing through wetlands, fertile plains, hills and mountains and it is traversed by many winter rivers that flow from the Troodos Mountains into the plains.

The UNBZ connects a patchwork of national forests parks, as well future Natura 2000 reserves. Since July 2007, the first scientific attempt to assess the flora and fauna has been undertaken in the Buffer Zone by a team of 14 scientists from the Greek and Turkish Cypriot communities. The study sites covered different habitat types, including river, coastal, farmland, wetland, and forest, with surveys of the flora and fauna, providing valuable information on the locations of wildlife corridors that could assist in prioritizing conservation planning for target species and habitats in the Green Line and the adjoining areas.[3] Some rare, endemic and vulnerable flora and fauna species were recorded, including the Cyprus Moufflon, on the verge of extinction a decade ago, and the Mediterranean Monk Seal, one of the most highly endangered species in the world today.

Cyprus also has its divided capital, Nicosia, where the Green Line bisects the historic core. The green pencil line that was drawn on a map in 1963 and that gives this border its name translates into reality on the ground as a "snaking, barbed-wire-flanked, muddy track (that) over the past 50 years, has had plenty of time to grow its own micro-culture and make its own history and experiences."[4] Cutting through the historic walls, the Buffer Zone disrupts the image of unity created by the perfect geometry of the Venetian fortifications, meandering along what was formerly the bed of the Pedios River before it became the main commercial axis of the city.

---

[3] Gucel Salih, Charalambidou, Iris; Gocmen Bayram; Karatas, Ahmet; Ozden, Ozge' Soyumert, Anif; Fuller, Wayne. *Monitoring Biodiversity of the Buffer Zone in Cyprus*. Near East University, 2007.
[4] Walker, Jane. *Green Line Culture*. April 22, 2004. (Unpublished)

Here, Nature disregards the Status Quo, with trees growing within buildings and plants spreading in the streets and on rooftops. The numerous pools of water remind us of the presence of the river, as do the wild flowers - the celandines and asphodels - that generally flourish along stream banks and in moist areas. Flash Floods that occur sporadically during the spring and summer months, causing considerable damage to properties bring back to our memory the historic catastrophe that occurred on November 10, 1330 in the heart of Nicosia, in which 3,000 citizens were drowned. More recently, on July 7, a severe storm resulted in the falling of 15 mm of torrential rain in 10 minutes, flooding the center of Nicosia and flowing into the Green Line, as if the former river was reclaiming its bed.

Water is regarded as "the second Cyprus Problem" after the conflict, and the island in increasingly suffering from severe drought. Rather than restoring the fabric of the Green Line thought should be given that the floods are partially due to the fact that the River Pedios was filled in and that there are less and less impervious surfaces to absorb water. The future uses of the Green Line should be based on a system of storm water management and catchment surfaces, to avoid flooding and to harness the great quantities of water the fall during the floods. This refers to a question of ecological landscape planning, which should become the foundation of all planning in the Green Line and beyond.

5. Learning from the Berlin Wall

Berlin was a divided capital city until 20 years ago. Today, in Berlin, if you have not "walked the Wall" when it was standing it is difficult to see the traces or to recognize its path. At times, the Wall is indicated by discreet signage, that is, a copper line or a strip of cobbles embedded in the pavement, but this linear representation does not convey the spatial impact of the wall and the death strip.

As the Cyprus Green Line is not one line, but two cease-fire lines defining a buffer zone, the Berlin Wall was not one wall, but a death strip surrounded by two walls. With retrospect, some inhabitants of Berlin feel that "the wall was dismantled too quickly" and lament that there are not more spaces to keep alive the memory. The first reaction of Berliners was to obliterate all the signs and scars of the Wall, but twenty years later, the city is fighting to preserve the last remaining segments. But we must not fall into nostalgia, or ostalgia[5] for the presence of the Wall. It is more interesting to reflect on the unique opportunity offered by the liberation of a military landscape within a city, looking back at the radical transformation of cities in the 19th century when fortifications were demolished and the terrains were used to plan infrastructures, green spaces, urban boulevards and new institutions, responding to the new needs of the city. What should be noted is that it is necessary to have a project and vision before the walls fall or are demolished, as the case of Berlin teaches us that once there is a solution, the economic forces of real estate quickly fill in the voids.

In the shadows of the more publicized and official Berlin Wall sites, some jewels of memory landscapes and pockets of green were salvaged along the necklace of the No-Man's land by local populations and organizations. These include the Mauer Park, a very popular green space between Prenzlauer Berg and Wedding, which resulted from a bottom-up, community led initiative; the Chapel of Reconciliation and Berlin Wall Memorial initiated by the Minister of the Evangelic parish whose land was swallowed up by the Death Strip; and finally, the Lohmuehle Wagendorf, an ecological community of caravan dwellers who have invested a segment of the former Wall.[6]

The members of the Lohmuehle community live totally off the grid, using solar and wind power, recycling water, and planting their own food experimenting with microorganisms to fertilize the earth and ward off parasites. It is both an ecological and cultural community,

---

[5] Nostalgia for East Germany or the former East Block.
[6] http://www.lohmuehle-berlin.de/

with an extremely low ecological footprint, where public concerts and artistic events are regularly hosted, and is probably the most visionary and experimental open space along the former Wall.

6. The Cyprus Green Line - from Vision to Reality

The Green Line project was first presented by the author to various stakeholders in Cyprus in 2006, including the UN, UNDP, and environmental NGOs.[7] The vision was inspired by historical and contemporary precedents worldwide, as well as by existing bicommunal cooperation between the two Cypriot communities. This project aims to engage all stakeholders and civil society in Cyprus and harness social, cultural and environmental collaborations between both sides that continue to flourish and that seek to overcome the conflict by building a sustainable future for all Cypriots. It will seek to provoke a shift from the narratives of disputed land rights and reclamations to common issues of preserving the environment and to act as a catalyst for the reintegration of the divided communities. As a backbone for the reconstruction and reconciliation process, it could become an opportunity for innovative environmental landscape and urban design and offer sites for the establishment of new organizations and institutions that will participate in overcoming the psychological rift.

---

[7] Grichting Anna and HPCR (Harvard Program for Humanitarian Policy and Conflict Research). *The Green Line of Cyprus: Human Development and Reconciliation through Environmental Cooperation*. Project Proposal, June 2006. Presented in Cyprus June/July 2006 to UNFICYP, UNDP, Reconstruction and Resettlement Council, Academic Institutions and a number of Environmental and Citizen NGOs.

The vision plan for the Green Line can also serve as communication instrument and as a tool to develop a legal framework for the implementation of the project. This vision should not be just a static representation of a post-conflict memorial landscape, but should embody a dynamic instrument to resolve the conflict, and should present an opportunity to "reframe the conflict," to act as a "consensus catalyst" that links environmental issues to the conflict resolution process, one that would require the involvement of environmental and spatial planners in the negotiation process.

In view of the many competing and diverging territorial claims that continue to divide the Cypriot populations, the feasibility of this proposal for the "greening of the Green Line" may be questioned.[8] The absence of political recognition between the two governments - despite ongoing talks - continues to impede formal collaborations between the two sides, but there are indicators in Cyprus and worldwide that environmental cooperation is being viewed as an alternative means to address the Cyprus problem and other conflicts.[9]

Cyprus faces many environmental challenges - including water scarcity, water pollution, coastal degradation, the loss of wildlife habitats - and this project offers an opportunity for Cypriots to collaborate on common goals. As well as the European Union, a number of intergovernmental agencies and nongovernmental organizations (NGOs) can readily be turned to for technical advice in establishing a transfrontier, or in the case of Cyprus, a bi-federal reserve: United Nations Environment Programme (UNEP), the United Nations Development Programme (UNDP), and the International Union for the Conservation of Nature (IUCN).

---

[8] *The Green Line may become Greener.* Article on the authors Green Line Project published by Sebastian Heller in the Cyprus Mail on November 29, 2009
[9] Ali, Saleem H. ed. *Peace Parks: Conservation and Conflict Resolution.* Cambridge and London: The MIT Press. 2007. (foreword by Julia Marton-Lefevre, Director General IUCN)

Naturally, there are many barriers to such a vision being implemented, the first being the question of the land ownership and the right of return of displaced populations, which has been at the centre of the Peace talks and one of the obstacles to a viable solution. But these obstacles could be overcome with anticipatory and timely planning and with the instruments that are used to create and manage state parks or to build highways and other public infrastructure, and it will be necessary to develop specific policies to implement the Green Line project. Amongst the tools of urban and environmental planning, Eminent Domain is an instrument of expropriation that can be applied to acquire land for public works and this would require that the environmental qualities and potential of the Green Line be valued as a public good.

Friends of the Earth Germany (BUND) have recognized, that land purchase is the only way to protect habitats from destruction in the long run, and they have started to buy unique habitats from private owners in six areas along the Green Belt. To this day, more than 10,000 people have become symbolic shareholders of the German Green Belt, having purchased around 280 hectares of the German Green Belt through Green Share Certificates.

2010 is the International Year of biodiversity. It also marks the 60th anniversary of the founding of the Republic of Cyprus and the beginning of the division of the island. Let 2010 be the year that we begin building this vision of a reunified island along the backbone of the Green Line, and let us begin to imagine this beautiful scar as a landscape of memory for the many victims of the conflict and as a haven for cultural and biological diversity on the "Island of Venus".

ENERGY USE AND ENVIRONMENT IN CYPRUS

Ali Korakan, President of Energy Engineers and
of the Energy Professionals' Association in Cyprus

Abstract

There are serious evidences for global warming. CO_2 levels rising in the Earth's atmosphere is one of the main contributors for Global warming and climate changes. Fossil fuel consumption has a significant role in CO_2 emissions.

Energy is one of the main driving forces of our society and fossil fuels are still the main energy source for the whole world. Cyprus is one of the countries that is and will be strongly affected by climate changes whereas the carbon footprint of the island and contribution to global warming is not so significant.

Although these concepts are fully mature within the community, the legal infrastructure is not established and is not in full effect to help combat global warming and climate change in the north of Cyprus.

In this presentation we will try to look at the relation of energy use and environment, why new policies are need, and what the new policies should include. This may be vision for the north of Cyprus.

1. Introduction

The international consensus is growing that the planet is facing irreversible climate change unless action is taken quickly. Climate change is one of the greatest threats facing the planet. If the earth's temperature rises by more than 2^0C above the pre–industrial levels, climate change is likely to become irreversible and the long term consequences could be immense. Low lying areas of the earth, including large parts of European countries, could eventually disappear under rising sea levels. Moreover, in many parts of the world there would not be enough fresh water to go round. Extreme weather events causing physical and economic damage would become more frequent. Economies could decline from cost of dealing with a different climate.

The above is the introduction paragraph from the booklet "Combating Climate Change", a publication of European Commission. Alarm bells are ringing for the environment, immediate action is inevitable.

2. New Challenges and their impacts

Global Warming, Climate Change, Renewable/alternative energy sources, green house gasses, CO_2 emissions, carbon footprint, low carbon economy, are subjects that we became very familiar and frequently encounter with in our everyday life.

There are serious evidences for global warming. CO_2 levels rising in the Earth's atmosphere is one of the main contributors for Global warming. CO_2 level in the atmosphere has reached almost to 400 parts per million (ppm). The upper safety limit for atmospheric CO_2 is 350 (ppm). Atmospheric CO_2 levels have stayed higher than 350 ppm since early 1988.*

Actually it all started about 200 years ago when human mankind discovered the energy value of carbon compounds deep in the ground. I don't know what these carbon compounds were called those days but nowadays we call them fossil fuels. Since the beginning of the industrial age, we have been excavating the ground to take out fossil fuels. Burning fossil fuels sends the carbon into the atmosphere in the form of carbon dioxide gas, and it will stay there for many many years. The carbon has moved from permanent storage underground in the earth to permanent storage in the atmosphere.

When the sun rays bounce off the earth, the layer of carbon dioxide acts like a greenhouse and reflect the rays back to earth. The atmosphere of the globe warms up like a greenhouse. Fossil fuel consumption has a significant role in global warming.

Oil consumption is responsible for 45% of CO_2 emissions. More than half of the total fuel consumption is used in transport. The world average is 52% and is estimated to be 57% by the year 2050. Cyprus has the same percentage with the world average. Coal, Oil, Natural gas is used for electricity generation. We use coal, oil, natural gas, and electricity in industry, buildings, space heating and cooling, lighting and the like. All these contribute to CO_2 emissions.

We are totally energy dependent. We need more and more energy to survive. The good news is that the world population growth rate started to decrease since 70ies, and is expected to continue going down in the future. This Means that the annual population change is also going down. However the world population is still increasing. It has doubled in 40 years from 1960 to 2000.

In parallel to the increase in population, energy consumption is also increasing. This graph is taken from Key World Energy Statistics published by the International Energy Agency. It shows the increase in energy consumption for the whole world. CO_2 emissions are also increasing in parallel with the increase in energy consumption.

The situation in Cyprus is not any different than the rest of the world. We have an increasing demand for energy. This graph is showing the energy consumption in the south Cyprus for the years 2000-2008.

Forecast show that this demand trend will continue. The graph shows forecast for the electricity demand of both North and South Cyprus.

The existing situation is not sustainable. This trend has to be reversed. UN and Governments of the world are trying to reduce GHG emissions. Kyoto Protocol is the well known protocol that is serving for this purpose. EU has already committed to reduce green house gas emissions by at least %20 by 2020. This is known as 20-20-20 by 2020 EU climate action which includes 20% renewable energy use and 20% energy efficiency. There are many programs that will help to achieve this target mainly by using energy more efficiently and switching to renewable energy sources. Intelligent Energy Europe is one of the main EU sustainable energy programs.

How are we going to reduce GHG emissions? The answer is Sustainable energy use. Two critical components of sustainable energy use are Energy efficiency and non-fossil fuel energy sources usage.

Sustainable energy policies require raising awareness since it all starts in our brains. Starting from civil servants, and children, public awareness should be raised for sustainable energy use.

- Not to waste energy,

- Buy and use energy efficient equipment,

- Always check the energy class of the equipment before buying.

- Never use resistive lighting (incandescent) or resistive heating elements.

- Use efficient lighting and heat pumps instead.

- Avoid peaks in our energy demands, transportation demands and all.

- Distribute our electricity consumption evenly to day and night.

- Support recycle schemes and programs.

We can save Energy, by using energy efficiently, using energy efficient equipment and machinery, reducing and recovering energy waste streams, fuel switching and the like.

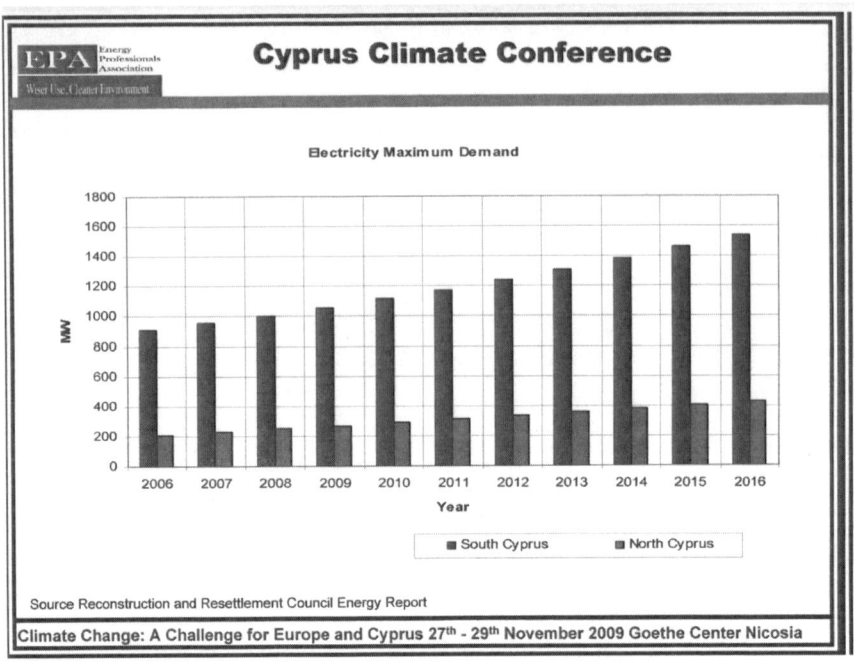

Climate Change: A Challenge for Europe and Cyprus 27th - 29th November 2009 Goethe Center Nicosia

Increasing the use of non-fossil fuel sources. Namely Nuclear, Hydro, sun, wind, wave, geo-thermal, geo-exchange, bio fuels, bio mass, biogas, wood etc.

Transport, Buildings, Power Generation and Industry are the four main consumers of "primary energy sources."

Transport has the highest percentage of primary energy use. The world average is 52 percent and is expected to increase to 57 percent by 2050. This is almost the same for Cyprus as well.

Sustainable energy use in transport requires:

Good town planning, distributing the city centers and market places and restructuring of the road infra structure to promote public transportation, providing safe routes for bicycle riding and walking.

Establishing adequate school bus systems and prohibiting parents to transport their children to schools.

Closing parts of the city to vehicle traffic, car pooling- reducing speed limits. Promoting by subsidy and taxation policies, energy efficient vehicle use, CO_2 emission per kilometer, hybrid cars.

Planning working hours for different groups with time lags to reduce traffic congestions.

Sustainable energy use in Buildings requires:

Architecture: Adapting principles of sustainable building systems in architecture, introducing extensive use of daylight, passive heating and cooling, shading, wall color choice and the like.

Solar day lighting will not only save energy and reduce CO_2 emissions but will also positively affect the health of the society.

Building Codes and labeling to define building energy performance.

Solar heating and cooling systems.

Energy Audits for commercial and industrial buildings.

Use of building management systems that will take care of efficient energy use for commercial and industrial buildings.

Cyprus is one of the rare countries to use solar hot water production since 1960s. However the system currently used is old technology from 60s and 70s. In this respect the efficiency of the so called thermosyphon type solar hot water systems are very low. Generally the tanks are located on top of the roofs, the cold water supply tank has no isolation and in winter the temperatures drop down close to 0^0C and the next day the system hardly recovers the heat lost during the night. Hence electricity is used to produce hot water. More efficient solar hot water systems should be obligatory. Maintenance is another important issue; solar panels should be cleaned regularly. Cyprus has a dry climate, more frequent cleaning is required. We can double the efficiency of even the existing non-efficient systems if we clean them regularly.

Conducting energy audits at commercial and industrial facilities will identify energy saving potentials and energy efficiency measures. These measures will save energy and GHG emissions when implemented.

Electricity Generation: Electricity is the highest form of energy. In this respect we are highly dependent on it.

The existing power generation technologies in Cyprus have the lowest efficiency around 30-35%.

Introduction of *"combined cycle"* power generation, heat and power cogeneration systems will reduce our primary energy consumption and reduce GHG emissions as well.

Combined cycle generation systems can reach up to 55% efficiency whereas Cogeneration systems can go as high as 90% efficiencies.

Renewable energy system investments should be promoted. Small PV solar power systems can contribute to power generation without any green house gas emission.

Energy Management is also vital for sustainable energy use. Energy management systems should be introduced to commercial and industrial facilities, energy accounting systems should be established and energy saving programs supported. There is considerable energy saving opportunities in industry. Energy audits should be conducted and energy efficiency measures should be implemented. Energy waste streams can be identified and recovered by Energy Audits. Equipment and machinery which are not efficient can be replaced with more energy efficient equipment and systems. Energy management systems should be obligatory for the industry. Saving the environment requires commitment. We must commit ourselves for the future.

INTERLINKAGES BETWEEN BIODIVERSITY CONSERVATION AND CLIMATE CHANGE

Horst Korn, Head of the Biodiversity Unit
of the German Federal Agency for Nature Conservation

Abstract

Climate change is affecting biodiversity and this poses unprecedented challenges to nature conservation. We will be faced to make choices and to set priorities. But biodiversity does not only suffer from climate change. It provides us also with a wide range of opportunities to enable human societies to better adapt to climate change and to buffer them against extreme events. Direct and indirect effects of climate change effect biodiversity but at the same time biodiversity is part of the solution when dealing with the problems of climate change.

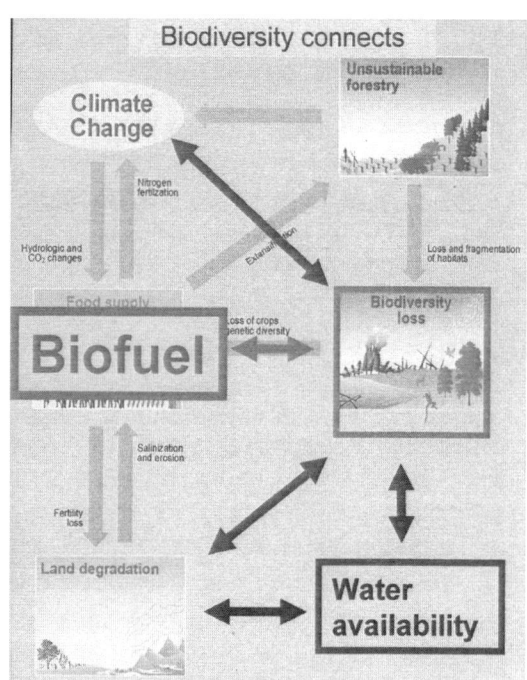

Many effects of climate change can already be observed in nature, like changes in seasonal and reproductive behaviour of species. It can already be predicted that fluctuations of populations will become more frequent, as weather extremes increase in frequency and intensity. However, population crashes occur less frequently in habitat networks that have stronger network cohesion. Temperature change, coupled with a change in the amount of precipitation and rainfall pattern will lead to a shift in the range of species.

Species with a small dispersal capacity and that are habitat specialists are more likely to decline than species that are habitat generalists and that have a large dispersal capacity. Because of habitat fragmentation, the effects of climate change on animals and plants will be stronger than just predicted by the temperature increase. The interaction between temperature rise and habitat fragmentation shows that species with a fragmented habitat are not able to follow shifting suitable climate zones.

To solve the problems of climate change that face both nature and human society's holistic approaches on the landscape level, involving different sectors of society are needed. Care has to be taken that well meant activities within one sector (like energy) do not counteract the targets of another sector (conservation and sustainable use of biodiversity).

Main Text

The relationship between nature conservation and climate policy has various sides. On the one hand, ecosystems are an important part of the climate system, mostly because of their role in sequestering, storing and releasing carbon. Terrestrial and marine ecosystems currently absorb a significant share of anthropogenic CO_2 emissions, while their degradation can lead to the release of large amounts of greenhouse gases (approximately one fifth of global anthropogenic emissions). It is thus clear that climate change mitigation policies cannot be successful without addressing the drivers of processes like deforestation, desertification or peat land degradation.

On the other hand, climate change has direct impacts on the structure and function of ecosystems, with consequences for the conservation of biodiversity and the provision of ecosystem services to society. Indirect impacts also exist – they are caused by human responses to climate change (such as increased use of renewable energy, increased efforts in prevention of natural disasters, changes in agricultural practices, etc.), which may have positive or negative effects on nature, depending on how they are designed. Strategies for adaptation to climate change therefore need to follow an integrated approach, in which nature conservation has to be both an independent topic and a cross-cutting issue.

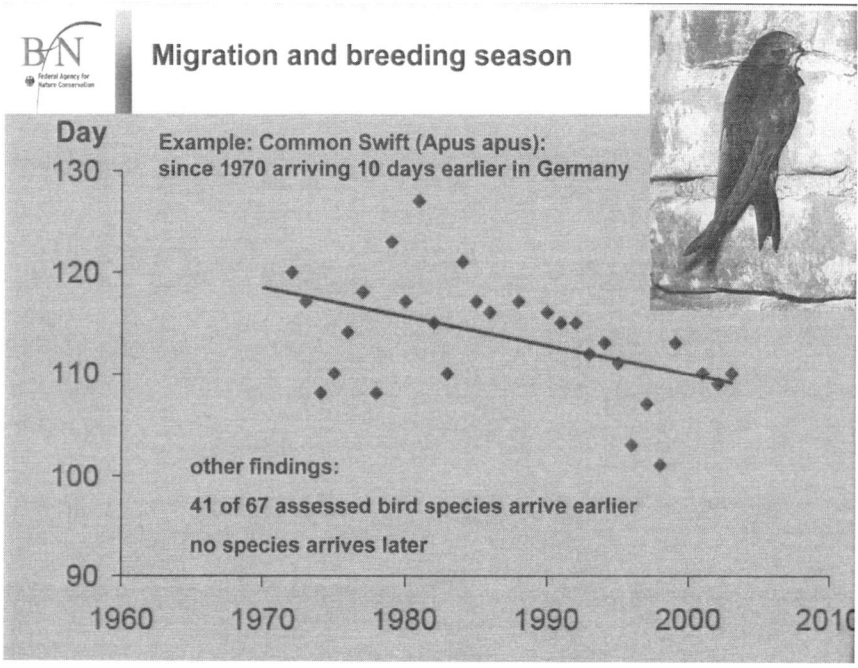

Many changes in animals and plant species have already been recorded:

- Changes in seasonal and reproductive behavior of species

- Shifts in "climate space" of species

- Changes in habitat composition as species move

- Increased extinction risk where population numbers are low, habitats are restricted or patchy, and climatic/geographic ranges are limited

57

- Spread of alien species. Some of them are invasive and become major pests for agriculture, forestry and fishery or may cause severe health problems in humans.

- Coral bleaching in tropical seas, which means that corals are dying in extremely warm water.

The implications for protected areas are:

- Protected areas are the last remnants of semi-natural habitat and the best places to maintain functioning ecosystems

- Focus for conservation management must shift from maintaining the status quo to managing dynamic systems

- Conservation objectives must reflect ongoing changes in species and habitats

- Climate change highlights the need for dynamic conservation designations

- Some issues for the role of the wider environment are:

- Protected areas will not accommodate all climate change impacts on biodiversity

- Many species will attempt to move to new climate space

- Habitat fragmentation restricts the movement of individuals across the landscape

- Climate change reinforces the need for landscape-scale connectivity/permeability

- Climate space projections can help in planning habitat mosaics to facilitate species movements

The role of nature conservation is to prevent climate change to further deplete our wealth of biological diversity. Major adaptation actions could therefore include:

- Assessment of climate change impacts through monitoring and modeling

- Management of ecosystems to optimize resilience and accommodate climate change

- Strengthening of partnerships between NGOs and government agencies, and of capacities for addressing climate change

- Identifying best practice cases and communication of advice and guidance

- Develop and implement "climate change proof" policies, plans and actions

To understanding the future: We need to keep working with models, but we must also recognize their limitations. They should rather provide us with scenarios than predictions, and we need to keep monitoring. To set our priorities and to decide on the right actions we need to categorize threats to habitats and species. And we have to focus on "no-regret actions" which may consist of

- The reduction of existing pressures.

- The increase in size of habitat patches.

- The increase of overall porosity of the wider landscape, to facilitate the movement of animals and plants (by seeds) and to avoid isolation of small, remnant populations with low survival probabilities.

- The creation of "what-if" areas; designed to allow natural processes to operate over larger areas (for instance new naturally functioning wetlands), as it will not always be possible to predict future biodiversity patterns

Many activities to combat climate change or to adapt human societies to the effects of climate change may be in conflict with the conservation and sustainable use of biodiversity.

Wind power poses threats to birds and bats and produces through heavy noise pollution when put at sea through vibrations and especially during the construction phase. They may also be in conflict with the issue of landscape aesthetics.

Solar energy only poses problems when put on the ground, instead of roofs and facades of buildings, thus potentially competing for space with other sectors like nature conservation and agriculture.

Hydropower changes the river flow and sediment load of running waters and cuts of migration routes of aquatic animals, like fish.

The so called bio-energy is the most problematic of all renewable energies, and not only because of severe competition for limited space and water resources for nature conservation and food production. To be economically feasible bio-energy is normally grown in huge monocultures (in woody plants often based on single clones), and in the near future it can be foreseen also with genetically modified organisms.

These plantations are characterized by heavy use of fertilizers and pesticides with all its environmental problems and which use a lot of energy to produce and to transport them. Because of the way bio-energy is often grown, the carbon balance is often negative or marginally positive. This is especially true when bio-fuels are grown on drained wetlands. To avoid further greenhouse gas effects bio-energy should only be produced from residues and waste but not from especially grown agricultural products.

Synergies between biodiversity conservation and climate change protection is possible but to terminate the most damaging practices so called "perverse incentives" have to be abolished or transformed into positive ones.

THE CLIMATE CHANGE – A CHALLENGE FOR THE WORLD

Eckart Kuhlwein, Chairman of the German-Cypriot Forum
and Member of the Board of German Friends of Nature

Abstract

As compared to 1850, global temperatures on the surface of the earth have increased by 0.84 degrees Celsius now already. While they were around 14.5 degrees, they have now reached 15.4 degrees Celsius. This is caused by increasing concentrations of heat-trapping gases in the lower atmosphere, the troposphere, through an incompatible energy supply, industrial agriculture, excessive mobility, and harmful chemicals...

Climate change radically jeopardizes welfare, peace, and safety on the earth. All in all, nothing less than the survival of human kind and the habitability of our planet are at stake. Within the next three decades the point of no return will be passed unless there is a radical turnaround. The goal today is to limit the global temperature increase to two degrees Celsius, but it seems that in Copenhagen the community of states will not agree on a specific goal.

Copenhagen will flop unless at least the following goals can be enforced:

The binding definition of a global reduction objective for greenhouse gases by 50 percent by the year 2050, which means that industrialized states will have to reduce their output by at least 85 percent, as compared to 1990.

Specific intermediate goals for a reduction of greenhouse gases for 2020 and 2030 and 2040 as well as a sanctioning of non-compliance.

Inclusion of the large threshold countries in the reduction goals, but a recognition that the industrialized nations are the major contributors.

Agreement on a global program with binding protection goals for the protection of ecologically important regions, such as soils, moors, forests and seas, in appropriate protocols.

A financing mechanism that provides for a global financial compensation between industrialized countries, threshold and developing countries.

An environment monitoring under the auspices of the UN, including a "security council" for environment and development.

Main Text

The earth has a fever: Humans are the virus that pushes up temperatures. Actually, this warning from the international climate science in February 2007 that startled the world wasn't really new. Since the mid-1980s science has been warning louder and louder that humanity needs to act so that a climate catastrophe may yet be avoided. There has been plenty of clear and hard evidence to show that the climate is out of balance, with the Intergovernmental Panel on Climate Change (IPCC) speaking of a probability of more than 90 percent.

The disease has been spreading faster and faster, and nobody will be spared unless some effective medication is given fast. What was felt to be a conceivable threat at the end of the 1980s, has become a real danger. The clock is ticking. The alarm signals have become too clear, and the evidence is overwhelming.

As compared to 1850, global temperatures on the surface of the earth have increased by 0.84 degrees Celsius now already. While they were around 14.5 degrees, they have now reached 15.4 degrees Celsius. This is caused by increasing concentrations of heat-trapping gases in the lower atmosphere, the troposphere, through an incompatible energy supply, industrial agriculture, excessive mobility, and harmful chemicals. They close the atmosphere's windows.

Humanity has been waging a "war against the atmosphere" (*Stephen Schneider*). The earth's weather machine has been shaken by the supercharging of the energy balance and the up-heavals in the chemistry and dynamics of the troposphere. This has far-reaching effects, not only through the warming, but also for wind conditions, the drying up of the earth, the stability of the marine systems, the melting of ice sheets, the distribution of precipitation and the vegetation of the earth.

This war against our natural environment was not only waged by capitalism but also by the "ton ideology" of communism that was only interested in simple, measurable results without considering the consequences. They were like hostile twins who tried the seemingly easy way of alleviating social conflicts through exploiting nature. That hasn't changed after 1989. On the contrary: Capitalism that has remained for now, keeps externalizing the social and ecological consequences of economic decisions at the expense of third parties, mainly at the expense of nature, the Third World and the future, even without its eastern opponent.

Climate change radically jeopardizes welfare, peace, and safety on the earth. All in all, nothing less than the survival of mankind and the habitability of our planet are at stake. Within the next three decades the point of no return will be passed unless there is a radical turnaround. Yet the discrepancy between the knowledge of the dangers and real actions has been increasing.

Even in the seventies there were anxious questions from the *UN World Meteorological Organization* (WMO) about the consequences of the high energy consumption and the related emissions of greenhouse gases for our climate. Together with the *UN Environment Program* (UNEP) the WMO founded the *Intergovernmental Panel on Climate Change* (IPCC) in 1988. The IPCC collects worldwide data on climatic processes and it examines scientific and socio-economic data. It also shows chances for avoiding problems or possible adjustments.

In 2007 the 4th status report of the Panel on Climate Change used an extensive cause analysis and complex calculation models on the future course of temperatures to state unequivocally that mankind is the main contributor to global warming. It said that it is "very likely that the greatest part of the warming observed since the middle of the twentieth century has been caused by the release of greenhouse gases by humankind". It also estimates the probability of a massive anthropogenesis climate change to be more than 90 percent.

Basically that was already stated by science in the mid-1980s. Even then the United Nations warned against a global temperature rise of 3 degrees Celsius by the year 2100, especially at the big UN climate conferences of Bellagio and Toronto. Since then scientific facts have been substantiated significantly. While there were only nine world scenarios at the beginning of the decade, the 4th status report of the Intergovernmental Panel on Climate Change was based on 23 highly complex computer models as well as precise paleoclimatologic research results and an extensive evaluation of specific weather data from approximately the past 150 years.

An increase by three degrees doesn't sound like very much at a first glance. But in reality it is a self-destructive experiment of humankind with the fragility of the earth. To give you an overview: During the past 600,000 years the global temperature only varied by ca. six and a half degrees Celsius – and only over a time period of ca. 100,000 years.

The lowest temperatures, during which the Alpine glaciers reached Ingolstadt on the river Danube in the north and Milan in the south, were around 10°C. The optimal climate which made the Mediterranean region a Garden of Eden, reached around 16.5° C. These shifts had serious consequences for life on the earth. The history of wars, migrations, poverty and misery must be seen in the context of climatic changes, too.

This time a lot more is at stake. The additional greenhouse effect caused by humankind threatens to add half of the climate change known in the past to the natural system. This means it comes faster and more radically than everything we know. And it does not only have to do with warming, for the climate change also changes humankind's living conditions dramatically: Hurricanes and floods, the spread of deserts and the deterioration of the soil quality, the melting of glaciers and the rise in the sea level. It results in famines, migration and inhospitable living conditions.

The value of a warming by 0.84°C poorly reflects the dramatic changes, for the climate change has a period of adjustment of between 40 and 50 years between cause and effect. To put it differently: It is only now that we feel the concentration of greenhouse gases that were concentrated up to the 1960s. A global rise by 1.5°C can no longer be prevented because in the past four decades the tropospheric concentration of the most important gases, carbon monoxide, methane, ozone or nitrous oxide has increased substantially. Also, it takes a long time for greenhouse gases to be reduced.

The regional effects vary greatly. The arctic region is hardest hit, with a distinct warming of more than 3° Celsius. In the ice and glacier regions the processes are especially pronounced. In Germany the warming of ca. one degree as compared to 1850 is a bit higher than the global average, and it is particularly pronounced in the Upper Rhine area, the German Alps and the North Sea.

When the public debate on the climate change started in the mid-1980s it would have been possible to limit the temperature rise to ca. 1.5°C. That goal is far from reality today, because it would immediately necessitate a far-reaching stop of industrial emissions as well as a comprehensive protection of soil and forests, of seas and moors.

The goal today is to limit the global temperature increase to two degrees Celsius, but it seems that in Copenhagen the community of states will not agree on a specific, let alone an ambitious goal. But the two degrees Celsius are already the Last Exit, and it is connected with serious consequences: Migration, poverty, food crises and, ultimately, a deplorable increase of violence

- In the Andes glaciers have decreased by 23 percent over the past 17 years. There, almost 100 million people depend on the outlets from the Andes glaciers for the

65

water and energy supply. Even today a reduction of the ice masses by two thirds can no longer be stopped.

- In Asia 635 million people live in low coast regions or river deltas. The changed riverine regimes and the rise of the sea level endanger the livelihood of ca. 40 percent of people living there.

- For Africa, with its almost one billion people, 230 million of whom are undernourished, a warming by two degrees Celsius would probably mean a 50% reduction of crop yields that are already poor anyway.

Economic profit seeking, old thinking and political idleness are the reasons why the global warming keeps increasing and many people will experience the disastrous results. And it will be getting more and more difficult to limit the warming to 2°C. Numerous scientists already doubt that this goal can still be reached.

Although the conference has been prepared for two years, Copenhagen threatens to become a disaster. An agreement is still a long way off. There only seems to be the question of who will be passed the buck. Like others, Denmark as the host country has been trying to save what may still be saved, but that is becoming less and less. The Danish government has suggested a "long-term counseling". The Copenhagen conference is to be extended to the next year, because big countries like China, India or the United States need more time to make decisions.

Of course, there has been some movement in those countries, too. The government in Beijing has realized the seriousness of the situation, because the changes have been felt increasingly in China, too. Floods have increased because the Himalayan glaciers that feed the large Asian rivers have been melting faster and faster. In Brazil the logging of tropical forests has dropped to the lowest level of the past 40 years. In the United States, too, there are strong forces that want more climate protection. That is to be welcomed, but it cannot replace a global climate protection agreement.

In Germany and the EU, too, all that glitters is not gold. The nineties were a lost decade, in particular:

- The cabinet decision of 1990 to reduce CO2 emissions in the old federal states by at least 25 percent by 2005 was clearly missed. In all of Germany (!) only minus 16 percent were reached.

- In Germany 2006 a 40 percent reduction by 2020 was decreed. In pertinent laws only 32 percent have been defined so far.

- During the time of the red-green government the then opposition voted against all laws and programs for climate protection – from the eco-tax to the law on renewables. But more should have been done during the time of the Schröder government.

- In the program of the Federal government against the economic crisis of 2009 only 13 percent of the funds were provided for ecologic investments.

Short-term thinking, selfishness and profit-making are still predominant. Some countries may do more now than before the IPCC report, but they only want to realize climate protection according to their laws and interests, not as a great and mutual effort of the world community. Abstractly they may support the goals of the UN, but they refuse to participate in specific agreements. This is still a fact: Politics lag far behind the ecological realities.

The result of this failure is an ecological colonialism that plunders the future. The United States are still mainly responsible for this. There, conservative forces are showing President Obama the limits of what he can do. In the United States 20 tons of CO2 are produced per inhabitant and year. If a global climate protection and global justice are to join forces which they should, the country will have to reduce emissions to one tenth of today's output.

The threshold country China, too, already produces an average of four tons per capita, which is twice as much as the globally acceptable amount of two tons. China has had growth rates of 10 to 15 percent per year. Power generation has been growing by ca. 100,000 MW per year, which almost corresponds to the capacities of all power plants in our country.

Even if the global game of poker around climate protection should stop in Copenhagen and specific measures and goals were decided upon, they would still lag far behind what needs to be done. But it doesn't even look as if a minimum program could be expected. Not concerning the overall objective by 2050, and certainly not where the specific intermediate goals for 2020, 203 and 2040 are concerned, not even for a global finance mechanism with the developing countries or the recognition of the protection of nature: Nowhere does it look as if a convincing agreement could be found.

It seems as if the world community has still not understood the full dimension of the challenge. Many play Russian roulette, hoping that their own country will be less affected than third world countries that are usually in regions that are ecologically sensitive. But that has little to do with the facts. Even the EU that was a motor of climate protection in the past years could not agree on a goal of a 30 percent reduction.

The world domestic policy will be put to the test. But it looks as if the industrialized countries, the main contributors to climate change, will be the ones who fail miserably in particular. Everywhere the resources of civil society, above all environmental, nature protection, and social organizations, need to be strengthened so the paralysis of politics can be overcome. What is to be done? Our time needs nothing less than an ecological revolution. Copenhagen will flop unless at least the following goals can be enforced:

- The binding definition of a global reduction objective for greenhouse gases by 50 percent by the year 2050, which means that industrialized states will have to reduce their output by at least 85 percent, as compared to 1990.

- Specific intermediate goals for a reduction of greenhouse gases for 2020 and 2030 and 2040 as well as a sanctioning of non-compliance.

- Inclusion of the large threshold countries in the reduction goals, but recognition that the industrialized nations are the major contributors.

- Agreement on a global program with binding protection goals for the protection of ecologically important regions, such as soils, moors, forests and seas, in appropriate protocols.

- A financing mechanism that provides for a global financial compensation between industrialized countries, threshold and developing countries.

- An environment monitoring under the auspices of the UN, including a "security council" for environment and development.

The countdown has begun adamantly with all the harshness of natural laws. Our world is at a crossroads. We will either have a century of ecology or we will have a century of violence and decline. That is where we are today. The map for a new progress has already been laid out, but it has not yet been fed into the navigation system. The central theme of sustainability will open a chance for a new way for Germany, for Cyprus and the European Union. Politics will now have to set the course instead of continuing to adjust and submit to economic constraints.

WATER RESOURCES MANAGEMENT IN NORTHERN CYPRUS

Mehmet Necdet, Head of Hydrogeology, Eastern Mediterranean University, Cyprus

Abstract

Cyprus is the third biggest island in Mediterranean Sea than Sicily and Sardinia. Character of the climate is mild winters and dry summers with very rare showers. Main economical activities are tourism, agriculture, light industry and universities. The island has a rich history and a natural beauty, although water resources are very limited. Usually semi-arid climate in Cyprus and the island's northern part of the character even more. Since the 1970s, a decreasing rainfall trend in the rate the other hand has been a significant increase in water demand. Negative developments in these conditions, groundwater levels drop, and lead the sea water intrusion in the coastal aquifers.

1. Introduction

Groundwater resources of the northern Cyprus are used for drinking, irrigation and other aims. The total groundwater abstraction can be estimated as between 85 to 100 million m^3 per year. Total amount for drinking or potable water supply for the villages, towns and cities are 20 million m^3; %90 of the remain is used for agriculture which is around 65 million m^3 per year.

Management of water resources planning is no case while the largest consumer of water in the agriculture sector in the amount of water consumed with the cultivated lands might be calculated. Ownership of water resources in Cyprus belongs to the public. The permit the use of water resources-related are authority of the District offices of the island colony of Britain in this way the period since the application is continuing.

Agriculture sector is the largest water consumer on the island. However, duties and powers of agencies responsible for agriculture in sustainable use of water resources are not related to a coordination mechanism. In the use of water resources for these issues is not taking into account. So that the island's two major groundwater resources have been intruded by seawater considerably and has significantly depleted. These groundwater basins are Southeastern Mesaoria and Morphou Aquifers.

2. The State of Water Resources

Hydrogeological features of Cyprus are quite well examined. Groundwater resources are replenished by rainfall over the island. The water resources in Cyprus are divided into four groups; Aquifers or groundwater basins, surface or pond water, purified sea water and treated waste water. Desalinated sea water is mostly used in Tourism by hotels located nearby the sea. The usage of the treated waste water is limited by now. Following major sources of groundwater in northern Cyprus are:

Kyrenia Range Aquifer, These are Mesozoic aged karstic limestone aquifers supply 50% of the water demand entire territory.

Upper Pliocene – Pleistocene aged Aquifers: This group is known as Morphou and Southeastern Mesaoria Aquifers. Morphou groundwater basin is built by gravel, sand and silt; Calcerous sandstones are the groundwater bearing rocks of Southeastern Mesaoria Aquifer. Those aquifers are also located southeast, northeast and northern coast of Cyprus.

River bed aquifers: These aquifers occur in river deposits in the western part of Cyprus. The age of the sediments can be estimated as Pleistocene to Holocene times.

Gypsum Aquifers: These aquifers are located in Mesaoria valley. The age of these deposits is Messinian.

Dams: Total capacity is 30 million m³ for all the dams. The use of dam waters is not efficient due to the gaps at the administrational level.

Treated waste waters: There is no efficient use of treated waste waters in northern Cyprus.

Main Groundwater Bodies in Northern Part of Cyprus

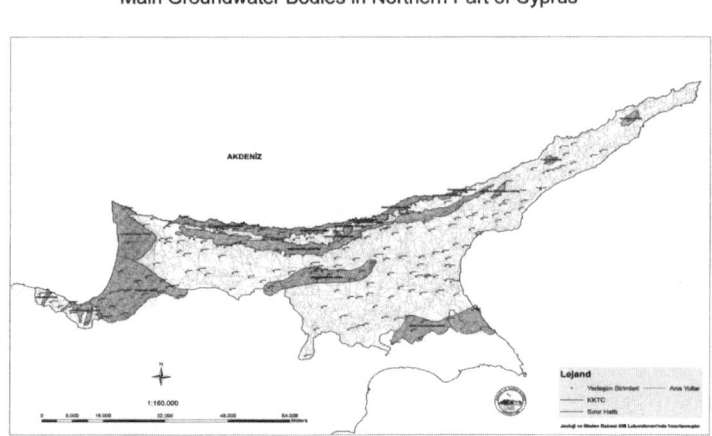

The depletion of water resources and quality degradation problems relevant the economic structure of agriculture is a predominantly in Cyprus. Economic structure based on agriculture, water resource consumption due to insufficient control of water resources in terms of quality degradation and to be consumed aroused results. Especially after the second world war modernization of agriculture taking place before the people by the power of the groundwater with diesel engine driven pump was replaced.

Provided incentives for the production of citrus in the beginning of the producers to have better economic conditions were targeted.

However, these applications are made without respecting the results of groundwater balance, such as Morphou and Famagusta groundwater basins intruded by seawater.

Famagusta coastline is almost entirely intruded by seawater today. The largest groundwater basin of Cyprus is Morphou which is gradually depleted. On the other hand 80 % of South Eastern Mesaoria Aquifer, the second largest groundwater basin, has already been depleted.

Primary drinking water source north of Cyprus is Kyrenia Range karstic aquifer. The water levels in this aquifer are lowered drastically year by year. The groundwater resources in Karpaz Peninsula are moving to the point of exhaustion too. A desalination plant was built at the sea side for the mass tourism plots of Bafra recently. This desalination plant supplies water also for the nearby villages.

3. What must be the Solution?

Short, medium and long-term plans should be prepared to be applied to programs and sustainable use of water resources should be provided.

Water use in agriculture be brought to the restrictions appear to be an ideal solution but anything before the water consumed in agriculture is under control and to counter the routing path, the network of the leak by determining the necessary measures should be targeted as a priority.

Use of treated water in agriculture should be prepared for the projects. In general, in particular farmers, community members should be educated in this field, these issues in their comments and suggestions should be taken into consideration. Agricultural sector in terms of using limited water resources should be analyzed economically. Water resources management and schemes will ensure the control of groundwater abstract should be prepared and implemented legal regulations. The existing water laws should be revised according today's conditions.

European Union water framework directive in accordance with the rules by drinking, swimming, water and waste water containing standard directives prepared law. This matter short - medium term measures must be in. As in the agricultural sector today who want more water instead of plant species, cultivation of less water should be encouraged to plant species. Small scale rather than large areas of land in agricultural production, more targeted projects should be prepared. The rate of water from dams on the hydrological conditions permit drinking purposes should be used for.

The poor quality water should be purified with technological investment for to be used. To prevent pollution of the groundwater basin, the necessary legal measures should be taken. European Union River Basin Management Plans must be foreseen. Urban plans must be compatible within the river basin management plans. Awareness raising campaigns within the conditions of water resources should be brought to public information.

4. Future Plans

European Union aimed to improve the environmental management capacity of the Turkish Cypriot community for the projects are implemented. These projects are to build waste water treatment plants for the cities in the northern coast of Cyprus.

Potable drinking water to the city of Nicosia in order to be awarded desalination plant, which will be built in Kumköy. Replacement project of the water networks in the cities is ongoing now. Water conveyance project from Turkey to Cyprus by pipeline is being designed.

INVERTEBRATE BIODIVERSITY OF CYPRUS

Özge Özden, Biologist, European University of Lefke

Abstract

There has been great concern within the scientific community about biodiversity loss and extinction crisis worldwide. It is known that there is an increasing rate of biodiversity loss worldwide especially within the global hotspots. The conservation of biodiversity has become a priority within the global hotspots. The conservation of biodiversity has become a priority within the Mediterranean region and globally. The conservation importance of an area can be determined by assessing its biodiversity.

During this research invertebrates were used as key species (indicator group) in order to assess the biodiversity in different ecosystems. Also population dynamics, abundance, species richness, and diversity of different invertebrate groups were identified. In addition to this, there are different groups of invertebrates used as indicators in order to identify the biologically valuable habitats for biodiversity conservation in Cyprus.

Main Text

There has been considerable debate within the scientific community about biodiversity conservation, as currently there exists scientific and public concern on the extinction crisis globally (Pimm and Raven, 2000; Brooks et al., 2002; Benayas and Montana, 2003; Gaston, 2005). There are numerous mechanisms of biodiversity loss and extinctions throughout the world, including: habitat loss or fragmentation, deforestation, agricultural practices, pollution, over exploitation, introduction of alien and invasive species, and climate change (Cincotta et al., 2000; Sala et al., 2000; Hodgson et al., 2005; Lewis, 2006). Biologists have identified 25 areas, called biodiversity hotspots, which are especially rich in endemic species and are particularly threatened by human activities (Mittermeier et al., 1998; Myers et al., 2000).

The Mediterranean region is recognized as one of the global "hot-spots", comprising some of the world's most unique biogeographical areas and harbouring high levels of biological diversity (Myers, 1990). The Mediterranean Basin comprises of beautiful mountain landscapes covered by scrub and woodlands, unique wetland areas, dune ecosystems and various agroecosystems (Blondel and Aronson, 2004). The mountainous landscapes, coastal hills and other ecosystems are home to approximately 25,000 species of flowering plants of which 1,300 are endemic (IUCN, 2003).

Unfortunately, anthropogenic disturbances are causing degradation of diverse ecosystems throughout the Mediterranean region. The most important causes of threat for Mediterranean species are habitat loss, degradation, pollution, overexploitation, natural disaster and human disturbance (IUCN, 2008). Tourism is having massive impacts, particularly on coastal ecosystems, and is considered to be one of the most significant pressures on biodiversity within the Basin (Nadin, 2008 and Cakan et al., 2005). The key major challenges on conservation of biodiversity can be defined as: Assessment, surveillance and monitoring of species and habitats, and also the detection of environmental changes (O`Connell and Yallop, 2002). Conservation biologists have developed alternative methods in order to monitor environmental changes in certain areas. One of these methods is the use of indicator taxa, which are species or higher taxonomic groups whose parameters, such as density, presence or absence, or infant survivorship, are used as proxy measures of ecosystem quality (Hilty and Merelender, 2000).

Cyprus is one of the "biodiversity islands" inside the one of the World`s hotspot areas (Myers et al., 2000 and Nadin, 2008). Cyprus is located in the north-eastern part of the Mediterranean region and its geographical location makes its fauna and flora both very interesting and diverse. The higher elevations of the Kyrenia mountain range support many endemic plants. Some of these endemics are red listed by the IUCN, such as *Delphinium caseyi* and *Brassica hillarionis* (Tsintides et al., 2007). Also the endemic orchid *Ophrys kotschyi* is commonly distributed along the Kyrenia Range Mountains and valleys especially in grassy places under Pines or

Cypress (Viney, 1994). These important endemic plants (*Delphinium caseyi, Brassica hillarionis* and *Ophrys kotschyi*) which are occurring along the Kyrenia Range Mountains are also listed under EU Habitats Directive (Annex II) (EC, 2004).

Cyprus is not only diverse in plants; it is also diverse in animal species. There are two endemic bird species that occur in Cyprus: Cyprus warbler (*Sylvia melanothorax*) and Cyprus pied wheatear (*Oenanthe cypriaca*). Cyprus warbler breeds on mountain sites in Kyrenia range, especially in bushes such as *Rhamnus oleoides* and *Calycotome villosa* (Bannerman and Bannerman, 1958; Flint and Stewart, 1992). The main negative effect on different ecosystems are large-scale building developments, quarrying activities along the Kyrenia range mountains, lack of a coherent and comprehensive regional development policy and also a lack of scientific knowledge regarding the existing biodiversity. Although, recently seven new Special Protected Areas have been declared by the local government in northern part of the island; the abundance, biodiversity of the plants, birds or the invertebrates are poorly known in the different ecosystems, both locally or even within the Special Protected Areas (Ozden et al. 2008).

In order to set priority targets for biodiversity conservation Cyprus, it is necessary to have a good, long term biological data. Although there have been several faunistic surveys completed in northern part of the island on different organisms (birds, mammals, reptiles and invertebrates), the only long term scientific research made to date has been on marine turtles (Fuller, 2008). There is a paucity of information regarding the ecology of insect fauna in Cyprus. The aim of this research was to identify the invertebrate biodiversity in different habitats and also to investigate the ecology of different taxonomic groups.

Firstly, field surveys were carried out over a two year period for the determination of thrips fauna (Thysanoptera) in the northern part of Cyprus. During the surveys 2029 specimens were collected. We recorded 43 thrips species belonging to 23 genera. Five genera and 14 species were new records for the island of Cyprus (Kersting et al. 2005).

Secondly, we determined the impacts of different management regimes on invertebrate fauna and diversity in Cypriot olive groves. We selected high and low altitude olive groves with no manage-ment, tillage only, or tillage – pesticide – fertilizer application. Dur-ing this study, 12,387 invertebrates were recorded and identified from 18 different orders or higher taxa. Our results showed that pesticide application on olive tree canopies significantly reduces the abundance and diversity of arthropods. We also determined the impacts of management regimes on woodlouse fauna. We found significant reductions in woodlouse abundance with tillage com-bined with pesticide and fertilizer application.

Thirdly, we used butterflies as an indicator group to identify the importance of forest and garrigue habitats for biodiversity conser-vation in Cyprus. Transect counts were used to assess the abun-dance and diversity of butterflies in old and young forests. We ob-served a significant effect of forest type on the abundance of butterflies. The number of butterflies and the number of endemic species was higher in old forests than young forests. Also we used butterflies to evaluate the conservation value of grassland and shrubland mosaics within garrigue ecosystems in Cyprus. Habitat type showed a highly significant effect on butterfly abundance, this was particularly the case with endemics. Greater abundance was observed during early and the late season in grassland habitats.

The results underline the potential conservation significance of agricultural ecosystems and should serve to promote ecologically sustainable agricultural production systems in Cyprus. Also as a result of this research, identification and protection of grassland-shrubland mosaics in garrigue.

EUROPEAN STRATEGY FOR RENEWABLE ENERGY AND CYPRUS

Mechtild Rothe, Former Vice-President of European Parliament, Cyprus Question and Energy Expert

Ladies and Gentlemen, Friends,

it's a real pleasure for me to be here in this meeting today. In the European Parliament I had all the years two main issues: Cyprus and second – renewable Energy. It is good to combine it!

We are now before the very important climate event in Copenhagen. Mr. Kuhlwein spoke about how important it is to achieve a binding commitment. Some days ago a Swedish Minister said on behalf of the EU-Presidency:

"The EU will work hard to achieve a result in Copenhagen that is a comprehensive, ambitious and binding agreement, with clear commitments for all the world's countries. There must also be a clear timetable and guidelines for putting the legally binding regulatory framework in place."

We in Europe are much further than in most other parts of the world. That's good. But it is not by chance that renewable energy has become a top priority on Europe's policy agenda. In 1997 - by the time of the European White Paper on Energy - the share of renewable energy sources in final energy consumption was 6.9%, 10 years later we approached a 9% share of renewable energy sources in Europe. This significant development was possible because of a strong commitment of politics, industry and civil society alike. And one of the key drivers for the promotion of renewable energy sources in Europe was and still is the European Parliament!

After the White Paper on Energy, which sets a target of increasing the share of renewable energy to 12% of Europe's total energy consumption by 2010 this target was filled with life by the "directive on the promotion of electricity produced from renewable energy

80

sources" in 2001. The directive sets an EU-wide target of 21% of renewables share in electricity production by 2010 including national targets for all Member States. Additionally, we adopted in 2003 the Bio fuels Directive setting a target of 5.75% market share of bio fuels in 2010.

Thanks to these reliable legislative frameworks and additional measures taken on the ground the story of renewable energy in Europe has become a true success story. And this success story has to be continued. Confronted with current challenges we have to sharpen our pencil and speed up to keep on writing the story of a truly sustainable energy supply in Europe.

Today, it is undeniable that the already ongoing climate change is caused by human activities - mainly by using fossil sources for energy purpose and thereby emitting tonnes of greenhouse gases into our atmosphere. Since the 1970ies greenhouse gas emissions have increased by 70% and CO_2 emissions from energy make up around 80% of all greenhouse gases. Who has any doubts about the negative impacts just has to look at the increase of heavy rainfalls and the decline of mountain glaciers. If we want to avoid the worst impacts we have to act now!

Ladies and Gentlemen, friends, we can contain its worst consequences by changing our energy policies. Our strategy has to be twofold: Reduce our dependency on finite conventional energy sources and increase our efforts to shift to an environmental, economic and socially sustainable energy supply. Today we know that there is a broad range of secure, clean and infinite energy source - renewable energy! Today we know that we have an enormous potential of wind power, of energy from geothermal, wave, tidal technologies, energy from biomass. We have an enormous potential of solar energy.

Ladies and Gentlemen, we all know by using renewable energy technologies an economic and ecological way of energy supply can be provided: They are unlimited, climate friendly and domestically available. With decentralized and even off-grid usable power production, renewable energy technologies offer a solution to the inevitable energy shortage that will face the developed world in the years ahead. They already offer the necessary answer to the challenge of climate change and environmental destruction - the answer to the potential disaster facing mankind in the future. And they can also offer power, light, comfort and economic growth to the developing world. By using renewable energy technologies an economic and ecological way of energy supply can be provided.

Ladies and Gentlemen, it is good to see that finally the Member States of the European Union are working together to tackle the challenges of securing access to energy and climate protection. Today we are much further. In 2007 – during the German Presidency - the EU adopted a strategy to steer a new energy policy for Europe. The 27 Heads of State endorsed unanimously to an integrated climate and energy package including three key goals:

First - binding reduction of greenhouse gas emissions by 2020 of 20% against 1990 levels - even 30% as part of an international agreement. Let us hope, that a clear agreement will be the result in Copenhagen. The industrialist countries have to take on its responsibility to go forward, to increase its efforts to reduce emissions of greenhouse gases. We know that the dramatic consequences of climate change will be felt most in developing countries. Second - binding 20% target for renewable energy by 2020 - including a binding 10% target for bio fuels Third - 20 % energy efficiency target by 2020. The three twenties are very important.

A new directive followed after this decision of the Heads of States. The EU has now a framework directive which includes the mandatory targets. The EU targets are translated into binding national targets for all EU Member States. The Commission based its calculation on a so called "flat-rate GDP-modulated approach". Based on the current state of share of renewable energy plus an increase of 5.5% for each Member State they modulated it depending on the GDP. In most cases, targets where set as well on the basis of already existing assessments or targets for the long-term. Here in Cyprus for instance a 9% target for the share of renewable energy sources in 2010 was already set. Now, the target for 2020 will be

13%. These binding national targets are absolutely necessary to provide for investors confidence and the common contribution of all 27 Member States to the binding common target of 20%.

Now some other important points of the directive:

1. Member states must sure that transmission and distribution system operators provide for either priority access or guaranteed access to the grid system. That's very important.

2. Interim targets and Renewable Energy Action Plans:

In the Directive we find an "indicative trajectory" for Member States shares of renewable energy in order to meet at least their overall target in 2020. So, these interim targets are just indicative. In order to make sure that all 27 Member States are truly progressing and to provide for investors confidence we need a reliable political framework. Due to the fact that we do not have sector targets for electricity or heating and cooling and that some Member States still tend to leave the decisions for the next government we urgently need a more binding nature of the interim targets!

Additionally, the Renewable Energy Action Plans are of major importance. We need the evidence that Member States are doing what they can - in the electricity, the transport as well as the heating and cooling sector. Member States have to state how much they want to do in the three different sectors and have to assess their domestic potential. They have to state which support they want to give to the different technologies. And they have to state how much of their national targets they want to meet by making use of the potential of another Member State.

What we need here is a clear template for the Member States. The negative experience with the National Energy Efficiency Action Plans - where some Member States even called the Commission asking what an Action Plan is - must be avoided by providing clear and detailed guidelines. The first Action Plans have to be tabled in June 2010. Last week EUFORES the European Forum for Renewable Energy organized a workshop for the writers of the National Action plans.

We are in Europe on a good way – but it is necessary to accelerate the process. By the way, today we know, that Feed-In and Premium Systems are the most successful support schemes for renewable energy. In a recent evaluation the European Commission made clear, that Feed-In systems - as for example the German "Feed-In Law" - are more effective and cost-efficient than "Quota-systems" for a real market penetration of renewable energies. In the meantime, a lot of Member States have adopted the principles of the German Feed-in system. Already today, 186 of 27 Member States have a similar law, which guaranties fixed prices for electricity produced from renewable energies. Even in India and China they used the Feed-In-System as a role-model for their own laws!

I am pretty sure that this success is as well the reason why in 2006 there was an agreement in the Republic of Cyprus for a New Enhanced Grant Scheme-setting in 2007 Feed-In tariffs for renewable electricity. And Cyprus has to do a lot.

The share of RES in the gross final energy consumption was 3.4 % in 2007 in the Republic. I have not a concrete figure for the North, but it could be a little less. The 2002 Action Plan gave support to the use of RES mainly to solar water systems therefore a development started.

The South is one of the leading countries in the use and construction of solar water heating systems. 92% of households are equipped with solar water heaters and 53% of hotels have installed large solar water heating systems.

But in 2020 Cyprus – and it is assumed that we have a united Cyprus – has to achieve 13% share of RES on the final consumption of energy.

Again – there is a lot to do. But it might be not a problem for the Cypriots. You have huge potential of renewable energy sources here in Cyprus. Sun, wind, biomass and others. It is good to hear that the new 82 MW wind farm near Paphos with 41 wind turbines will represent almost 3% of Cyprus's requirements and that 14-million Euros have been earmarked from for the development of the energy sector in North Cyprus and that the amount will now be used on investments for the use of solar energy. Just some words have to be said to the second pillar of sustainable energy – energy efficiency.

After the energy service directive we got some days ago a compromise for the recast of the building directive. The cheapest and easiest "source of energy" to get is energy efficiency and energy savings. Energy efficiency measures not only help to reduce Europe's greenhouse gas emissions, but to reduce our energy import dependency as well. 20% to 30% of Europe's energy consumption could be saved by using our resources in a more efficient way. And buildings are responsible for 40 % of energy consumption and 36% of EU CO_2 emissions. In Cyprus – for example – is the energy part for cooling more important than for heating. I was very delighted that the first prize of the Energy Globe went in 2008 to Cyprus for the" first zero energy house of North Cyprus". Activities like this are full in line with the new Energy Performance of Buildings Directive. Nevertheless - pilot projects are very important but not enough. Until 2020 all new buildings have to be nearly zero energy buildings and the remaining energy need has to be covered through renewable sources. Additionally the Member States have to find ways for the transformation of existing buildings to fulfill the standards as well. So, a lot to do. But it is absolutely necessary to do it. Thank you!

WATER PROBLEMS IN CYPRUS

Pantelis Sophocleous, Environmental Engineer,
Project Supervisor for the Water Resources Management

Setting the Scene

The climate of Cyprus is Mediterranean with average annual rainfall of 460 mm. However, in the last 30 years the annual rainfall has fallen to approximately 350 mm.

The average annual potentially usable water resources in Cyprus amount to 370 million m^3. This includes water from four sources: surface flows, groundwater, seawater and purified water from sewage treatment plants. Surface flows are about 127 million m^3 in total, stored in dams. Underground aquifers and springs provide about 139 million m^3, including an excessive demand of 29 million m^3. Two seawater desalination plants produce some 40 million m^3 per year. Purified water in limited quantities, used in agriculture and in many cities and communities in Cyprus, is coming from wastewater treatment plants. The re-use of treated wastewater is expected to increase significantly over the next few years.

The total annual water demand is around 267 million m^3. Most years there are shortfalls in water production, causing water shortage problems. To give an idea of where water is used, 69% of water goes to agriculture, 29% in drinking water, a small amount for environmental purposes, and an even smaller amount in industry.

Problem Analysis

Due to the fact that the annual usable water resources are not sufficient for the ever increasing needs of the island, the Ministry of Agriculture, Natural Resources and Environment, took the decision to extend the existing desalination plants as well as to create additional plants. The water produced will mainly cover the needs for drinking water. The construction and operation of these units create two major problems. On the one hand, increased pollutant emissions (currently energy consumption of about 3.5% of national electricity) and on the other hand, increased water fees under the new pricing system (cf. EU Water Framework Directive 2000/60/EC).

The lack of adequate water resources creates additional problems. The national economy of the State as well as agriculture and ecological habitats are adversely and directly affected. Tourism in Cyprus accounts for the largest industrial revenues. Without an adequate quantity and quality of water, the island's hotels will be directly affected. This will have a significant adverse effect on the national economy, with repercussions on society. If too much water is used for tourism industry, not enough would be left for agriculture, leading to possible desertification of the island. The lack of water also leads to the decline of fauna and flora of Cyprus and this could potentially be irreversible.

Rain in Cyprus – Disaster or Gift of God?

In October this year, there was severe flooding in several areas of Cyprus. The causes of floods are varied. Some are detailed below:

1. Climate change is causing the phenomenon of sudden and intense local storms;

2. The often unnecessary and widespread sealing of natural soil roads reduces the porosity of the soil, causing the flow of rainwater in the residential streets to have nowhere to go;

3. Failure to create adequate channels to cope with rainfall in urban areas;

4. The numerous natural streams with concreted culverts have very small dimensions that may not have the capacity to cope with the volume of storm water;

5. Taking all the above into consideration, there is a considerable risk of flooding in urban areas since the rainwater cannot seep into the ground.

6. An inadequate number of retention basins contribute to unregulated flows in case of heavy rains.

It is our proposal that specific discussions should take place on preventing flooding and storm water management in urban and rural areas of Cyprus; involving experts specialized in water management and environmental issues.

Excess in winter – Shortage in summer?

Our rivers are used as dumping grounds. In order to avoid uncontrolled dumping, the Ministry of the Interior has appointed 17 inspectors. However, it would appear that personal or loyalty issues are put before official responsibility.

We respect and support the approach that the polluter pays!

Based on the results of our assessment we feel the responsibility for the avoidance of uncontrolled dumping should rest with the municipalities. As an example let us take the municipality of Geri. The current situation is that is has 1,000 m3 of solid waste. When we check in 3 months time, we will find a further 500 m3 of waste. Our proposal is that the municipality is responsible for this environmental pollution. For waste relocation one will need about 50 trucks in case each carrying 10 m3. Based on a unit price of 500 EUR per truck, the municipality would have to pay a total of 25,000 EUR.

On the other hand, if the municipality takes responsibility, say, 500 m3 of the original 1,000 m3, it can reclaim the costs incurred from the government.

Our Strategy for Solving the Water Problem in Cyprus

As things stand, we believe that a review of the water policy of the Republic should be carried out immediately, looking at the two following scenarios:

1. Today divided; and

2. a future united Cyprus.

The Republic of Cyprus should be able to identify and determine the characteristics of a river basin throughout the republic. This would be an important practical element of a peaceful policy towards the Turkish Cypriot community.

The following immediate steps are proposed with a view to an optimal water resources management policy:

Set up a centralized water agency to further review the current water policy, in particular to optimize water resources management.

Promote specific dynamic simulation models in major water control projects:

• Calculate the flow of rain in residential and non-residential areas.

• Optimize the surface area of dams in order to find a balance between evaporation and precipitation...

• Assess the quantity and quality of groundwater bodies through artificial recharge using treated wastewater and avoiding seawater intrusion risk.

3. Monitor and assess water losses in water supply system, in particular to improve the networks in order to reach less than 5% water losses.

4. Guarantee sufficient flow velocities in pipelines (vmin = 0.5 m/s) in order to prevent settling of solids in the pipeline. This would avoid the frequent cleaning of the pipes.

5. Encourage the installation of home treatment units for individual homes, as well as promote the use of rainwater in each house. Encourage the installation of units for reuse of gray water.

6. Take control of all drilling (mostly by farmers), even private boreholes (in rural and residential areas).

7. Review current policy on the creation of golf courses. Stop the government offering licenses to build golf courses.

8. Promote environmentally friendly detergents for cleaning cars without using water, especially large fleets of vehicles, especially in public service, army, police, and fire.

Sufficient Water for Every Household in Cyprus!

In Cyprus, the rainfall is not sufficient. Water is essential to life, growth, development and progress. The storage of fresh water is limited. The rainwater – a gift of nature - could replace precious drinking water, contributing to the constant management of storage.

The rainwater is mainly gathered from house roofs via water gutters. This water is stored in a small stern, in which mud and gravel concentrates at the bottom. Furthermore water can be stored in another tank and distributed for gardening using a water pump. Therefore the replacement of precious and expensive water could be achieved with no cost. In a medium size residence with roof area of 200 square meters, we are able to gather up to 100 cubic meters annually (with a minimum rainfall of 350 millimeters per year).

The Gray Water is gathered from wash basins, showers, baths, washing machines and other domestic appliances. It is stored and processed with the effective technology of brace-system. Furthermore the water is recycled for toilet use. This water could be used effectively for cleaning and gardening purposes. Using this system, Pantelion saves you at least 50% of your drinking water per day. In a residence of four people (using 100 liters per habitant per day) saving approximately 200 liter per day, the Pantelion system could provide you with storage of up to 70 cubic meters of water per year.

ELECTRICAL ENERGY
IN THE NORTHERN PART OF CYPRUS

Ayşe Tokel, President of the Chamber of Electrical Engineers

Main Text

Electrical Energy is the most important way of meeting energy demand in the world. Today it governs the economy and it is an important factor for the human development and a modern life.

The main resources related with the generation of electrical energy in our world are Natural Gas, Coal, Nuclear, Hydro and Renewables. These energy resources are used for the generation of electricity.

This is the percentage usage of the resources: Coal 26,6%, Hydro 6,30%, Nuclear 6,00%, Crude Oil 36,8%, Natural Gas 23,4% and other 0,90%. We see in the percentage usage, that the energy supply is still dominated by fossil fuels, which give off greenhouse gasses when we burn them for energy.

Different types of power plants are used to produce electricity. Each country uses a different mix of resources.

Thermal Power Plants

In a thermal power station the prime mover (turbine) is steam driven. Heated water turns into steam and moves a steam turbine which in turn drives an electrical alternator. Thermal power plants are widely used around the world to supply a majority of the energy demand. These plants consume ***fossil fuel*** (e.g. *coal*, *fuel oil* or *gas*). It is the burning of fossil fuel, that heats up the water and gives us steam.

In North Part of Cyprus, electrical energy is generated using thermal power plants. This is the only source to cover the electricity demand for the time being in North Part of the island. Thermal Power Plants have negative impacts on the environment such as:

Heat produced in thermal power plants are released to the environment.

The cooling effect that is done with the water around the plant results in increased temperature of the surrounding water.

Thermal Power Plants cause acid rains.

There is a high level emission of greenhouse gases.

Nuclear Power Plants

Nuclear power is generated from controlled nuclear reactions using radioactive materials, like uranium. These power plants use nuclear fusion techniques. Electric utility reactors heat water to produce steam, which is then used to generate electricity. These plants work exactly the same way as Thermal Power Plants except nuclear reactors are used to heat the water instead of burning fossil fuel.

Nuclear power plants that do not function properly may cause fatal problems like in Chernobyl. In this environmental disaster, tons of radioactive waste material was released to the atmosphere. No nuclear power plant is 100% secure. This is why it needs to be under the control of experts so a high level of safety measures has to be taken. The radioactive waste, which is harmful to the environment, needs to be under observation for many years, and has to be kept in a safe way to make sure that it does not contaminate the nature.

Hydroelectrical Power Plants

Hydroelectrical power plants utilize the energy in falling water and convert it into electricity. A simple mechanism is used for this process. Water is directed to channels for free fall. The flowing water turns the turbines and they rotate the coupled alternators and electricity is generated. Hydroelectrical power plants with a reasonable design criteria are built on the rivers in the areas with adequate rain. Sufficient slope for water fall is needed. Hydroelectrical power plants are environmentally friendly. But unfortunately in our country this does not seem to be applicable because of the lack of water in our island.

Geothermal Power Plants

Geothermal Power Plants are another alternative renewable resource that can be used.

Geothermal source is the accumulated heat within the earth's crust. The presence of this accumulated heat at various depths of the earth's crust heats up the existing water resources to high temperatures. As a consequence steam and gasses are released. Geothermal energy can be utilized either directly or with in-direct means. Electrical energy can be generated where the temperatures of the geothermal liquids reaches 2000 degrees Celsius or higher. As a general trend in the world, generation of electrical energy from geothermal resources is increasing every day.

Solar Power Plants

Solar power plants convert the energy particles in the sun light to electrical energy. Photovoltaic cells are used in large dimensions at solar power stations. The materials like *crystal silicium* and *gallium arsenite* are used in the production of these photovoltaic cells. These power plants are renewable, sustainable and environmentally friendly.

Wind Power Plants

Wind power plants are used to generate electricity out of blowing winds. The wind blows on to the rotary wings of the system and rotates the shaft which is coupled to an alternator. This in turn generates the electrical energy. So this is yet another renewable, sustainable and environmentally friendly system.

Generation of Electricity in Cyprus

We already mentioned about the existing energy resources and electrical energy generation methods in the world. The most commonly used resource for generation of electricity in Cyprus is fuel oil. Considering the negatives of this kind of production, new power stations need to use alternative resources that are more environmentally friendly. Existing sustainable energy resources in Cyprus are sun and wind. Sun and wind can play a supplementary role to the main production. They have zero "fuel cost" and are environmentally friendly.

That means the urgent need to invest in Renewable Resources in our country.

"Every house is a possible power station"

This is the slogan of our Chamber of Electrical Engineers.

Conclusion

A balanced mix of energy resources need to be used in electricity production. Alternative sustainable energy resources need to be part of electricity production in our country. This urgently requires the modification of the appropriate laws on the subject. Energy Efficiency laws also needs to be worked on which should help the "Demand (Load) Side". Reduction in electricity consumption means reduction in production which automatically helps the environment.

MODEL PROJECTS
OF ENVIRONMENTAL COMMUNICATION AND EDUCATION

Ulrich Witte, Head of Environmental Communication,
German Federal Environmental Foundation

Abstract

Since its foundation in 1991, the Deutsche Bundesstiftung Umwelt
(DBU) supports pilot projects in the fields of environmental technology, environmental research and nature conservation, and environmental communication and protection of cultural assets. Nearly
360 of the approximately 7,500 projects are outside of Germany.

Environmental communication as one of the central tasks of the
DBU aims to raise public environmental awareness and to commu-
nicate environmental knowledge. In this sense the foundation supports exemplary projects targeting a positive influence on people's
behavior. The DBU activities in the field of environmental communication cover a broad spectrum - from supporting school activities
over the development of environmental education and the organization of exhibitions, the support of digital information media, and
of artistic forms of expression.

Ten current examples from selected fields - biodiversity, climate
change, energy consumption and research – show that different
target groups, especially children and teenagers, can be addressed
with creative concepts and that economy and ecology are not contrary to each other.

1. First Example

To correctly classify the example projects presented in the following will require first an explanation of the Deutsche Bundesstiftung
Umwelt DBU and its "philosophy".

The foundation was established in 1991 on the initiative of the then Federal Government. Privatizing a state-owned steel group generated around 1.25 billion euros, which formed the capital of the newly founded Deutsche Bundesstiftung Umwelt DBU. From the interest of this capital, around 7,500 projects were supported with a total of approximately 1.3 billion euros to date. At the same time, the endowment has grown to around 1.8 billion euros.

Student Companies in the Context of Education for Sustainability

- Project partner:Regional Environmental Education Center Hollen
- Business areas
- Qualification programme
- 13 student companies from three Bundesländer
- Funding € 251,000

DBU ⟨ᴼ⟩ Deutsche Bundesstiftung Umwelt

The foundation, whose funding focuses on small and medium-sized enterprises, states as key eligibility criteria the terms "innovation", "model" and "concrete environmental relief." Early on, the DBU has committed to "Sustainable Development" as it had been decided at the UN Summit in 1992 in Rio de Janeiro. Although the foundation resulted from a governmental initiative, it is a private foundation according to civil law. The interaction with the state level is indicated by the composition of the board of trustees that is appointed by the Federal Government, with several senior functionaries of the legislature and executive among its members.

The funding range of DBU can be taken from the organization chart of the foundation, showing the three departments environmental technology, environmental research and nature protection and environmental communication and protection of cultural assets, and assigning them to different areas of support. About 90 employees deal with the processing of projects, mainly received in the form of concrete applications.

The promotional activities of the foundation are largely nationally oriented, approximately 95% of the projects relate to Germany. The foreign activities - about 360 ongoing projects - center on Central and Eastern Europe. In exceptional cases, the foundation is also active outside of Europe and has supported, for example, projects in the U.S., Japan, the Philippines and Africa.

2. Second Example

The promotional activities of the DBU in the field of education and information transfer are assigned to the department "Environmental Communication and Cultural Assets". One would expect that environmental communication is something like the public relations work of an environmental foundation; however, it is something else. The term of environmental communication exists in Germany now for about 20 years. It is a comprehensive term covering all activities within environmental issues. Whether the exchange of ideas or information on environmental problems and possible solutions as part of private conversations or the mass media coverage, or on behalf of state institutions, whether in the form of a book, brochure, or a lesson - all these levels and forms apply to environmental communication. So the DBU supports projects under the umbrella of "environmental communication" that serve the teaching of environmental issues.

In this sense, for example, we support concrete activities at schools, the creation of digital information media, events, the building of environmental facilities, the establishment of environmental museums, exhibitions, etc., including the implementation of competitions, theater productions and artistic creations. Target groups and partners implementing these projects are widely diversified:

organisations and associations, municipalities, universities, schools, companies, etc. Around 70% of the activities are directed to the young generation, to children and teenagers.

We distinguish between environmental communication and environmental education. In disseminating information, the media play the leading role, whereas teaching support keeps the environmental education on living. In "real life" the projects usually reflect both aspects.

According to our self-image, environmental awareness and knowledge are fundamental conditions to practice environmental protection and anchor it in the daily life of people, in economic activities or in political decision-making. Environmental awareness and knowledge do not arise automatically. Exemplary projects in different sectors of the public serve to maintain environmental awareness on an advanced level and to influence people positively in their behavior - even if a good knowledge not automatically entails good action.

The Earth Summit of Rio de Janeiro 1992 enriched the vocabulary of environmental protection with an important term that has become an integral part since then: the Sustainable Development. Environmental education is increasingly developing in the direction of "Education for Sustainable Development", linking the aspects of ecology, economics and social issues. Contemporary environmental education should be seen in the context of sustainable development and must be measured against the aspects of sustainability.

3. Example Three

The pilot projects described below are current and exemplify the commitment of the DBU in particular problem areas.

One of the most pressing environmental problems is the massive loss of biodiversity around the world. To counteract this, we need a targeted communication in education and information, especially to the younger generation. This need is in some contrast to the declining interest of children and young people for issues of conservation.

In order to draw the attention of young people to the topic of biodiversity, the competition "Discover the Diversity of Nature" addresses young people from 10 to 14 years in schools, associations and organizations. They should explore valuable ecosystems and natural areas in their regional and local environment - even in the city - and propose measures for their conservation. A network of experts and environmental information centers offer advice to the young people, their competition entries can be either analytical scientific or artistic-creatively designed. The winners of the first phase of the competition were awarded last year by the Federal Minister of the Environment.

A strong international approach to the subject of biodiversity for young people provides the International Wilderness Camp Falkenstein in the core zone of the Bavarian Forest National Park. Several buildings of indigenous groups from different continents serve as accommodation for young people during environmental education programs. The implementation of these programs in the wilderness area of the national park and the original experience with the typical accommodation of other nations allow for a broad educational approach, considering besides typical issues of biodiversity also cultural and social implications in terms of sustainable development.

Children and young people are the main target groups for the environmental communication of the DBU, about 70% of all activities aim at the younger generation as a "hope of tomorrow". The project "School Labs" adapts a special German problem context. Germany is known for its leading role in technology, but it is increasingly said that the "technical offspring" is missing and the interest of young people in natural sciences decreases. Keeping in mind that significant problems of environmental protection, such as energy issues, are insurmountable without any technical innovation, the program "School Labs" connects the scientific interests of young people with the environment. The building of student research centers, teaching laboratories and research stations at schools, universities and training centers is supported to advance the topic of "research for environmental protection".

The initiative "Sustainable Student Companies" is about to bring young people to the reality of working life and advance their interest in environmental protection. Students companies are small enterprises in schools that are independently run by the students, and where real money is made (which then is used for school, education and environmental protection purposes). The concept combines the focus on working with the frequently raised demand for a stronger economic teaching of basic skills in school.

Core of the project is the training of teachers and students in the sense of classical corporate governance (from legal questions over business models and managerial costing to warehousing and advertising) in order to translate this knowledge in the own student company. Such companies can be, for example, a catering service for organic food, a travel agency for sustainable school trips, a school's workshop for bicycles (as opposed to the motorized school traffic) or a recycling service for electronic devices. The project approach is pedagogically suitable even for students who have problems with the classical teaching at schools.

Not children and teenagers but consumers are in the focus of the project "ZweitSinn" - a broad-based sustainability project in the best sense. Old furniture is used as a resource for the production of exclusive new furniture with a contemporary design. Decisive is the close cooperation of various schools of design and of so-called recycling centers, where the products are collected and usually people work in the context of social projects, and of cabinet makers. The newly designed furniture in modern design are communicated through special exhibitions, fairs and other initiatives, and show how existing resources can be used a second time (ZweitSinn).

Climate change and its challenge to mankind is the outstanding environmental problem of our age. For a long time ago it is no longer a question of how climate change can be prevented, but how to deal with its already observed impact, and how to avoid an increase of more than 2° C in global warming. The exhibition "2° C - Weather, Man and his Climate" in the renowned Dresden Hygiene Museum is one of several climate exhibitions of the DBU, which will be presented with different priorities and for different audiences in different German cities. The exhibition in Dresden is aimed specifically at children and young people and uses new media such as computer animation, laser installation or Internet portals to attract the interest of young visitors.

Who wants to solve the problem of climate change must deal with the theme "Energy". In addition to the replacement of carbon-based energy with renewable energy, the so-called energy efficiency plays a major role. The DBU developed a large campaign "Haus sanieren - profitieren" <Profit from refurbishing your house> with the aim to motivate private house owners to an energy-efficient renovation of their properties. Most of the single-family houses in Germany, which were built after World War II, meet no longer current requirements of an efficient use of energy. Core of the campaign is a large-scale training program for craftsmen to offer private house owners a free initial consultation. It is expected that through this project approximately 675,000 tonnes of CO_2 savings and investments of almost 1 billion euros can be activated, which will help both economy and ecology.

Environmental problems cannot be solved only at a national level, they generally do not stop at national borders. A close cooperation with neighboring countries is not only in Europe useful and necessary. The project "Environment Builds Bridges" centers international cooperation and shared responsibility for environmental protection. The project brings together some 5,000 students and 34 schools from the Czech Republic, Germany, Hungary, Poland, Slovakia and Slovenia. Students from these European countries explore together with German partner classes environmental projects and environmental issues and report as student journalists in major newspapers on special pages. The project teams or classes visit each other in the course of one year. This project involves 20 major

European newspapers, and the state presidents of the countries involved took over the patronage for the project.

Appropriate structures are required to keep the environmental awareness and environmental knowledge permanently high. In addition to the improvement of teaching at schools, environmental education plays a major role even outside of school. The DBU has supported some 60 environmental education centers in their structure, a special emphasis was originally placed on the former GDR or East Germany. Here, too, it was essential to promote exemplary projects with innovative contents, methods or concepts. A well-known project is "Burg Lenzen" which was inherited by the largest German environmental organization BUND and has become now a very attractive venue.

An old weak point of environmental protection is to focus too much on insiders and not to inspire the broad population for "green" ideas". Here, compelling and attractive examples are often better than long-winded speeches or dry literature. For more than five years, the DBU supported the project "Sport and Environment" in order to attract sportive people for environmental protection and nature conservation. The sports sector in Germany offers ideal access possibilities, since almost every second German is organized in a sports club. In close cooperation with major sports organizations, individual climate protection and nature conservation projects have been supported with the aim to show people a good environmental solution for their own private area. Modern energy technology has been installed in many sports facilities in order to drastically reduce the consumption of water, heating or light. Supported were also projects that showed the design of sports facilities under the aspects of nature conservation, such as golf courses and water sports facilities. Particular attention received projects that show how sports can be organized so that arrival traffic, energy consumption or waste generation can be dramatically reduced. The few project examples clearly show that it is possible to influence people positively in their behavior through communication, education and knowledge. This is the ultimate goal of all education efforts - changing behavior. The examples show further that even creative approaches are successful. And they show that ecological and economic thinking are no diverging interests but combine synergistically in many cases.

Edited by Deutsch-Zyprisches Forum e.V. (DZF)

Chairman: Eckart Kuhlwein
Bramkampweg 5, D-22949 Ammersbek

Mail: kuhlwein@naturfreunde.de

Copyright Deutsch-Zyprisches Forum e.V. 2010

Charts and Fotos: Sofoclis Aletraris, Michael Bender, Ibrahim Karabardak, Ali Korakan, Horst Korn, Mehmet Necdet, Özge Özden, Ulrich Witte

www.cyprus-climate-conference.info